INDIAN TRADE
GUNS

Pioneer Press Union City, Tennessee

INDIAN TRADE GUNS

1982© Pioneer Press, Union City, Tn. 38261
All rights reserved
ISBM 0-913150-43-6

CONTRIBUTORS

Warren W. Caldwell

S. James Gooding

T. M. Hamilton

Charles E. Hanson, Jr.

R. T. Huntington

Carl P. Russell

Carlyle S. Smith

Arthur Woodward

John Barsotti

SPECIAL ILLUSTRATIONS BY

John Barsotti

Carl P. Russell

ACKNOWLEDGEMENTS

This book, INDIAN TRADE GUNS, was first published in 1960 as a collection of archaeological research papers by the Missouri Archaeological Society. The editing and compilation of the individual paper was, at that time, done by Mr. T.M. Hamilton, a member of the Society.

After its distribution to the members, the manuscript and all photographs, negtives, etc, were relegated to the attic. It sat for several years until Nancy (Bagby) Merz took the manuscript and began to work it into a book for commercial distribution. Mrs. Merz (then owner and publisher of Limbo Library of Taos, New Mexico) had the work to the point that all new typesetting had been done and pages were pasted up . . . in fact, it was ready to print. At this time, Nancy moved from Taos to Portland, Oregon, and the book was again put aside.

In 1979, Mr. Hamilton wrote to Pioneer Press about contacting Mrs. Merz to perhaps obtain the manuscript and the publishing rights to the book. This was done, and obviously, an agreement was made between the two publishing companies.

My personal thanks to Nancy Merz for the work already done on the manuscript. It has made the job much easier and has saved many hours of extra work.

Also, thanks to Mr. T.M. Hamilton, who brought the book to our attention and who helped in many ways to bring about an agreement with the officials of the Missouri Archaeological Society.

A special thanks is extended to the men who contributed their knowledge and expertise to this publication:

Warren W. Caldwell	S. James Gooding
T.M. Hamilton	Charles E. Hanson, Jr.
R.T. Huntington	Carl P. Russell
Carlyle S. Smith	Arthur Woodward

and to: John Barsotti and Carl P. Russell for their special illustrations.

CONTENTS

ILLUSTRATIONS

INTRODUCTION

Most of the information appearing here is timeless and will continue to be as pertinent tomorrow as it is today. S. James Gooding's study on the sale of trade guns by the Hudson's Bay Company is a mine of information to which the reader can always refer with confidence. The factual findings of Charles E. Hanson, Jr., Carl P. Russell, Warren Caldwell and others are of as much interest now as they were in 1960 when they were first written.

On the other hand, some of my own contributions are of a more speculative nature, so additional information gained during the intervening years has either modified or augmented them. If the reader is aware of this and they lead him on to other readings, he will then have a broader understanding of the subjects than if he only had the most recent publications at hand.

For instance, I am as puzzled today as I was twenty-two years ago by the 18th Century smoothbore barrels with bores of .50 and smaller. I no longer think they were or French origin, but I cannot say with certainty that they were English. Possibly they were Spanish. The standard bores mentioned in the French documents of that period are .32 and .28 *calibres.* This means that they were designed to shoot lead balls weighing thirty-two to the *livre* (with bore tolerances from .55 to .599"), or twenty-eight to the *livre* (.577 to .623"). At no place have I found where guns were ordered with bores smaller than .32 caliber. There was a judicial opinion handed down at Rochelle in 1749 concerning a supplier who furnished trade guns with bores as small as .38 *calibre* (.525 to .571") in filling an order calling for .28 *calibre* (.577 to .623). The supplier was required to replace them with barrels of the larger .28 calibre bore.

We do not yet know as much about 18th Century English trade guns as we do about the French, but by the 19th Century, the nominal bore was 24 gauge. (.579").

The Malta Bend Gunsmith's Cache was, in all probability, limited to the tools listed on page 32, plus a few of the better cocks and more complete locks. My experience since writing about that find leads me to the conclusion that the majority of the stripped lockplates, broken cocks, and the fusil barrel with the tang hammered down against the breechplug, were discarded items picked up the young LeFaivre on the village site proper.

Nothing can detract from the distinction due John Witthoft for first bringing to our attention the fact that there were two distinct types of gun flints used in Colonial America; those made by cutting long flakes into short sections, as described in the translation from the French by Carlyle Smith (pp. 161-188); and, an earlier type made by striking spalls from a prepared core or nodule. My article (pp. 189-196), based upon information given me by Mr. Witthoft, is the first where these "wedge-shaped spalls" are described and discussed in an historical context. This aroused much interest, and considerable research on these gun flints followed.

Witthoft eventually published a comprehensive study in which he concluded that the spall-type gun flints were made exclusively in the Netherlands,[1] but this only aroused more discussion. Finally, Seymour de Lotbiniere of Brandon, England, showed beyond question that the English had been making these gunspalls throughout the 18th Century.[2] Briefly, de Lotbiniere agrees with Witthoft that until the closing years of the 18th Century, England used the new style French gun flints, whenever she could get them; but, with the reservation that most of her fighting was done with the old spall gun flints which she had been making since the invention of the snaphaunce in the 1600s. Incidentally, we know from the excavation of old English forts and campsites that they were surprisingly well supplied with the French gun flints, but how the British Board of Ordnance managed to get them, even during the American Revolution, is one of those mysteries which remain to be solved.

The manufacturing technique described in detail (pp. 161-188) by Dolomieu and Gillet-Laumont was not published until the closing years of the 18th Century, and well after the English had finally learned the French secret. Just how the English finally discovered the technique is not known, but de Lotbiniere, in a story published in the MINNESOTA ARCHAEOLOGIST, (May, 1980, pp. 54-69) shows that the first English gun flints made by the French "flake" process were offered to the British Board of Ordnance in 1775.

It is interesting to note that the French succeeded in keeping their technique secret for over a hundred years, for a Canadian archaeologist, Jean-Francois Blanchette, has found those French flake-type gun flints on a campsite which had been covered by a landslide in 1663.[3]

Many of the basic problems involving the French and English gun flints made from flakes have now been solved, so present research is concentrating more on the earlier forms. We know very little about the very earliest gun flints because so few examples have been found and identified. As for the spall-type gun flints which immediately preceeded those made from flakes, we now definitely know that both the French and the English were busy making them by the hundreds of thousands from about 1650 to 1750. The question is, how to tell one from the other???

Dr. K.O. Emery of the Woods Hole Oceanographic Institute, discusses the petrographical differences between flints mined in England and those mined in France, in a paper entitled "The Geology of Gun Spalls", in my book, COLONIAL FRONTIER GUNS, pages 148-153.

T. M. Hamilton
Miami, Missouri
May 22, 1982

1. Witthoft, John (1966) "A History of Gun Flints," PENNSYLVANIA ARCHAEOLOGIST.
2. de Lotbiniere, Seymour (1977) JOURNAL OF THE ARMS AND ARMOUR SOCIETY, England
3. Blanchette, Jean-Francois (1975) HISTORICAL ARCHAEOLOGY, pp. 41-54.

I
INDIAN TRADE GUNS

CHAPTER 1
THE TRADE GUNS OF THE HUDSON'S BAY COMPANY
by
S. JAMES GOODING

In the early years of the second half of the 17th Century, Medard Chouart, sieur des Groseilliers, and his wife's brother-in-law, Pierre Radisson had had considerable success trading with the Indians of New France. On their return to Montreal they encountered difficulties and their valuable cargo of pelts was confiscated by unscrupulous officials. They left New France for New England and then went to England where they were successful in influencing Charles II and his cousin, Prince Rupert, in a trading venture in the New World.

In 1668 the men set out for Hudson's Bay in two ships, *The Eaglet* and *The Nonsuch*. Radisson's ship, *The Eaglet*, almost foundered in a storm and returned to England while Groseilliers continued alone. Groseilliers returned to England in 1669 with an impressive cargo of furs. Other trips were made in the following years and at the same time a company was formed. On May 2, 1670, it was granted a charter addressed to "The Governor and Company of Adventurers of England Trading into Hudson's Bay."

1

Des Groseilliers, and more particularly Radisson, exerted considerable influence over the decisions of the newly formed Hudson's Bay Company. They were both experienced traders who had lived and traded with the Huron, Iroquois and Algonquin Indians of New France. Radisson was consulted on numerous occasions about what type of beads, combs, flints, mirrors, and guns would be most suitable for Indian trade.[1] Because of this, and because of the background of the two, it is quite likely that there was considerable similarity between the French Trading Companies and the Hudson's Bay Company.

The use of firearms by the Indian is of inestimable importance to the historian. But the question "How many guns did it take to change their way of life," is one which is extremely difficult to answer. As early as 1641, when theoretically, no one would sell a gun to an Indian, the Iroquois approached the French with the attitude that they "Had to have arquebuses to eat."[2] This was undoubtedly an exaggeration intensified by their desire for arms to wage war, but it does indicate that they were to some extent dependent upon them.

At a later date, in 1857, when testifying before a royal commission on Hudson's Bay, Dr. King stated "that it requires a whole lifetime for an Indian to learn to approach an animal close enough for the bow and arrow."[3]

The intention is not to estimate the number of guns in the hands of the Indians of North America at any given date, but to show approximately how many guns were delivered to the Hudson's Bay Company for sale to the Indians. From this, other historians may some day be able to estimate the number of guns distributed by the other companies and thus evaluate the influence of firearms in their area for any given date.

In addition, the names of the gunmakers who worked for the Com-

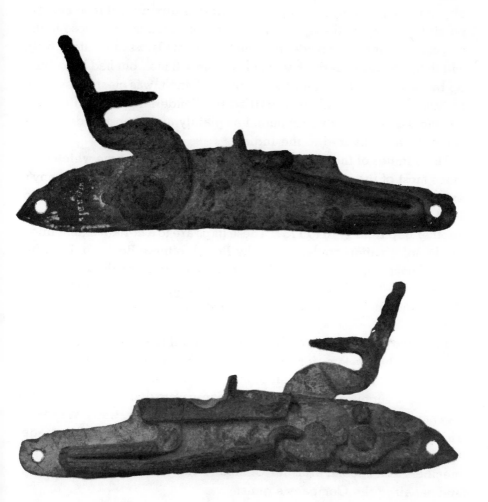

Figure 1. Flintlock made by Anthony Morris, found near Thornhill, Ontario, Canada.

Morris made seventy-five guns for the Hudson's Bay Company in 1692 and forty in 1693. This lock, heavily encrusted with rust, was cleaned and the Morris mark could be read.

pany may date a gun part; which could be the only means available of assessing the date of a given Indian village. It was by means of this list that the lock illustrated in Fig. 1, p. 3, was known to have been made in 1692 or 1693. To be useful it is necessary, of course, to be able to read the name of the gunmaker or to find some other identifying mark. This is not as impossible as it may seem. Even though an iron or bronze object is very heavily built up with corrosive products, it is sometimes possible to remove these, leaving a surface which is very close to the original. An iron knife blade from the ossuary at Ossossane (dated 1636), which has an original thickness of less than 1/8 inch but had been built up by the action of rust and corrosion to 3/8 inch, was cleaned by electrolysis, using the method described by Plenderleith.[4] When cleansed, the maker's mark was stamped as plainly and almost as deeply as when it was delivered to the Indian.

The minutes of the Hudson's Bay Company—the source which provides most of the information for the first 200 years of the Company's existence, are, unfortunately, not complete. Those of the years 1671 to 1674 have been preserved but then there is a gap until 1679. There is another gap from 1718 to 1737. These gaps are to a certain extent filled by the information contained in the Rough Minute Books and the Invoice Books. Here, then, are the primary sources for the material in this article. They have been supplemented by the Company's Letter Books, Indent Books and from the journals of some of the different posts.

From the earliest days of the Company until the last half of the 19th Century, the system for purchasing guns remained unchanged. Anywhere from one to sixteen gunsmiths contracted to produce guns of a pattern supplied by the Company. These were delivered to the Company and were inspected by the Company's gun viewer, who was usually also a gunmaker. He did not manufacture guns for the Indian trade although it was usually he who supplied the arms for the ships and crew members and special arms for Company employees. He also cleaned and repaired the Company's guns.

Guns are mentioned from 1671, but it is not until 1674 that they were described by name. On March 19, 1674, John Shaw, William Boulton (who in 1673 had served as the Company's gun viewer)[5], Jos. Stacey, Thomas West and Edward Ireland were paid varying amounts for "Fowling peeces a 21s. peece . . . Guns at 20s. p. gunn . . . Snaphans Musqts at 10s. p. peece."[6]

4

With the resumption of the existing minutes in 1679, references to firearms became more frequent. Unfortunately though, there is nothing definite which would describe any particular arm. It is necessary to piece together the short instructions given to the gunsmiths or the gun viewers to determine when each characteristic was introduced.

The earliest guns are described as being five feet long. This possibly refers to the overall length but later references to length indicate that it is the barrel rather than the overall measurement which is meant. Guns of four and a half and four feet were introduced before 1680 and between then and 1684, a three and a half feet length was added to the guns available. Between 1690 and 1693, there were orders for guns of three feet but they were not ordered again until 1717. In 1693, there were seven guns five and a half feet long ordered. Orders for guns of this length were not repeated, and there were no further shipments of the five feet length after 1684. In 1798, an initial order of 25 guns with two and a half feet barrels was sent to Fort Albany. It was repeated in 1800, and apparently sold well for the quantities increased over the next few years.

Between 1670 and 1700, the Company had a number of "experimental" guns made up which were to serve as patterns. On January 21, 1680, it was:

> Ordered that Mar. Stacy, Palmer, Powell and Sanderson Gunsmiths doe prepare each of them Three Gunns for Samples of 4 foot 4½ and 5 foot which they are to prepare at their own charge to be returned if the Committee shall not like them, that we may Employ such of them who use to make the best work.[7]

At the meeting held on January 28th, these guns were presented and the Secretary wrote:

> Mar. Craddock and Mar. Phipps desired to consult with some pson. who knowes the Country, whither the three patternes which the gunsmiths have left with their names each upon his owne Guns be good and propper for the service of the Company and the gunsmiths to attend againe on Munday next.[8]

On November 14, 1681, Samuel Oake, a gunsmith who had worked for the Company in Canada from about 1675 to 1680, was ordered to present patterns for guns "which are fit for the country" and again in 1682 reference is made to the "pattern gunn of Hardeman."[9]

It appears that previous to 1680, the guns were not marked with the maker's name, for at that time the defective guns returned from the bay were distributed in "proporsions" to the gunsmiths for repair.[10] In this same reference it is inferred that in future the gunsmith's names will be marked on their guns. This is borne out by the reference of

January 28, 1680, but it is not specificially mentioned until the minutes of March 2, 1681, when 250 guns were ordered from William Palmer and Joseph Stacy.[11]

The lock, which is probably the most important part of a gun for identification purposes is, unfortunately, the part about which we know least. In addition to the reference quoted above where fowling pieces, guns, and snaphance muskets are mentioned, we have the following:

January 20, 1682—Those locks that are wanting must be round.[12]

December 5, 1683—Agreed with Mr. Stacy and Pickford for plaine guns att 30s. by gun the samples of whc., are Sealed wth, the Compa. Seale whc. are not to have any flaws, cracks, brasses and are to be made of curred Iron, round locks of 3 holes, the Screw Nailes and trickard hardned the stocks not glewed but varnished.[13]

February 23, 1693—Also the following Instructions are ordered to be given Mr. Powell Viz:

To pass noe Brazed Bar nor any Peeced Stocks.

To stampe noe barrll nor Locks with ye Compa marke that are not every way good and perfect.

To make use of ye compa stamp only on the barrll and stocks which are for the compies use.

That every Lock either of gun or pistoll have the makers name thereon.[14]

From this we learn:

1. The locks must be round. Towards the end of the 17th century, lockplates with an oval or rounded cross section came into vogue. This is undoubtedly what is referred to in this order, and determined the form of the lock which was to remain in style for trade guns for the following 200 years.

2. Locks of three holes. The earliest flintlocks were fastened to the stock with three screws. The foremost came through under the frizzen spring, the middle, under the hammer or between it and the pan, and the rear near the tail of the plate. By 1683, the three screw attachment had made way for the two screw on civilian guns.

3. Each lock had to have the name of the maker upon it. In the reference to the name of the gunmaker being marked on the gun quoted above, it did not stipulate where the name had to be marked.

4. All other information concerns the quality of the guns. On one occasion, the Company complained to the makers that the quality of arms was not up to the contract specifications. When the gunmakers pointed out that the increase in the cost of iron made it impossible to comply with the contract, the Company increased the price which they would pay so that the quality of guns would not change.[15]

The characteristic large trigger guard of trade guns was probably introduced about 1740. The minutes for December 24th of that year state that orders were given to Abraham Jones, the Company's gun viewer "To acquaint all the gunmakers that the guards be made larger than usual."[16]

It has not been possible as yet to place an introductory date on the typical brass Dragon-shaped sideplate. Beginning with the annual order of guns for 1748, the minutes specifically mention that the sideplates must be polished. This order is repeated with almost every purchase for the next ten years. We cannot be certain that this refers to the cast brass dragon plate but there is a very good possibility that it does. This is emphasized by the fact that the armourers' stores for 1746 included an item known as "fish skins," though it is not certain that "fish skins" and the brass dragon plate are the same item. At least one question arises about the above assumption. Ian Glendenning, in his book *BRITISH PISTOLS AND GUNS, 1640-1840,* illustrates a dragon shaped sideplate found on a pistol by T. Green. This is the same Thomas Green who was appointed Company gun viewer in 1717 and in March of that year was ordered to make pattern guns of four feet and three and a half feet lengths "to be standards, for the gunsmiths to make the others by."[18] The Dragon plate is too similar to disregard!

The only remaining point of interest is the name of the North West Gun. As Hanson has pointed out this name predates the formation of the North West Company.[19] No mention of the North West Gun as a specific type has been found in the early minutes of committee or in the instructions to the gunmakers or the gun viewer. In 1761 though, among the list of tools requested by the armourers working in the Bay are two short sentences which indicate the North West Gun was a very definite type at the time. Previous to 1761, the references to guns and hunting guns as different styles of firearms are quite common. In addition there may have been a third type described as a fowling piece. This difference is only evident in the writings of the employees in Canada. It does not appear in the orders to the gunsmiths. In the armourers indent for 1761, however, the gunsmith requested:

Britch Screw Plate and Taps for Britching Gun Barrels of the same thrd as the NW Barrels are.

Boreing Bitt same Size as the NW Guns have for boreing the hole for the ram rod.[20]

This is the earliest reference found to date which shows that the North West Gun had emerged as a definite entity. The name appears with increasing frequency so that by the middle of the 19th Century, almost all trade guns were called by that name.

THE COMPANY MARKS

Apparently there were various Company proof or viewers marks in use at different times. It is possible that the gun viewers used their own mark to indicate that the guns had been inspected by them, or the viewer's mark may have been used in conjunction with a Company mark. Unfortunately, there have not been enough identifiable Hudson Bay Company guns found from the period being dealt with to draw any definite conclusions, but there are a number of points worth recording.

In the minutes of March 30, 1685, it is noted that the secretary was ordered to:

"Enter the Compa guns imported from Amsterdam as ye African Compa doe. This committee have resolved to Compa Goods shall be marked in the future with the marks as in ye margin."[21]

The mark which the secretary drew in the margin is shown as "A". (Fig. 2) The same mark or a slight variation of it was put on the crates of guns for shipment. This was also drawn in the margin of the shipping lists and appeared from then until sometime after 1725.

The mark "B" (Fig. 2) was found on the 1780 lock by Wilson (Fig. 3). The original impression was not too clear and the effects of time have not improved it, but the lower left portion retained enough detail to make the drawing.

The mark "C" (Fig. 2) is the familiar sitting fox over the initials EB found on most 19th Century Hudson's Bay Company guns.

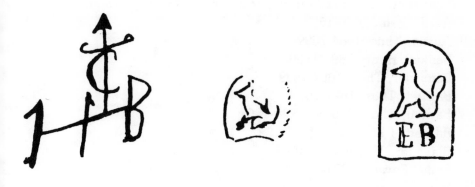

Figure 2. Identification marks on guns.
ITEM A: The mark which the Secretary drew in the margin of the minutes for March 30, 1685.
ITEM B: The mark found on the Wilson lock of 1780.
ITEM C: The sitting fox over the initials EB found on most later HBC trade guns.
ITEM D: Brass sideplate from the flintlock pistol by T. Green who was the HBC viewer in the first quarter of the 18th Century. This is an extremely early example of the serpent sideplate which became the trade mark of the 19th Century trade gun. *By courtesy of Cassel & Co.*

GUN MAKERS AND THE DATE OF THEIR CONTRACTS

* Viewer. Many viewers later became Company gunsmiths. The
  dates shown include both capacities when this happened.
  Arkill, Peter 1695-1699
  Austin, Thos. 1684-1699
  Bankes, Henry 1694-1699
  Bannister, Thos. 1684-1699
  Barnett, Thos. 1821-1867
  Barnett, Thos. & Sons 1821-1867
  Barnett, J.E. & Sons 1821-1867
  Blaymier, Henry 1674-1682
* Bond, Edward 1771-1784
  Bond, Edward
  1822-1873
* Bond, E. & W.
* Bolton, Wm. 1671-1674
  Bradt, ---- -1687
* Brazier, John 1761-1767
  Brazier, Frances 1768
  Brooke, Robert 1678
  Brooks, Ed. & Son 1852-1854
  Buckmaster, Jos. 1745-1763
* Bumford, John 1750-1775
  Carlisle, ---- -1684
  Dyer (or Dyon), Richard 1694-1699
* Ermindinger, James 1684-1688
  Finch, John 1684-1691
  Gale (or Galo), Chas. 1691-1697
  Godward, Edward 1693-1699
* Green, Thos. 1715-1728
  Green, (Widow) 1728-1729
  Grimmington, Michael 1689
  Hardeman, Mathew 1678-1682
  Hartwell, John 1683-1691
* Hatcher, John Cottrell 1764
  Hawkins, John 1695-1699
  Hawkins, John Sr. 1715-1727
* Hawkins, John Jr. 1717-1718
  Heylin, Joseph 1775-1777
  Ireland, Ed. 1674-1675

* Jones, Abraham 1730-1748
* Jones, John 1737-1750
  Joyner, Ann and Steven Sandwell 1774
* Joyner, John 1764-1774
  Kerby, Henry 1694-1697
  Kiplin, Chas. 1693
  Kiplin, Chas. 1728-1735
  Kiplin, Mrs. Hester 1736-1737
* Law, Edward 1691-1695
  Loader, Richard 1697-1699
  Morris, Anthony 1692-1693
  Nelson, John 1691-1699
  Nicholson, Ed. 1687-1712
  Nollon, John 1691
  North, Edward 1757-1760
* North, Edward 1769-1770
  Nutt, Wm. 1715-1716
  Oakes, Sam 1682
  Palmer, Wm. 1674-1681
  Parker, Wm. 1837-1875
  Parker and Co. 1837-1875
  Parker Field and Co. 1837-1875
  Parker Field and Sons 1837-1875
  Peddell, James 1688-1722
  Phillips, Thos. 1727-1732
  Pickfat, Chas. 1737-1757
  Pickfatt, Humphry 1715-1725
  Pickford, Humphrey 1682-1697
* Powell, Thos. 1682-1700
  Richardson, Michael 1685
  Sanderson, Lawrence 1680-1682
  Sandwell, Stephen 1775-1777
  Shaw, John 1674
  Sibley, John 1692-1714
  Silk, Robert 1678-1700
  Smart, Franc. 1715-1717
  Smart, John 1721-1727
  Smith, John 1687
  Stacey, Joseph 1674-1690
  Staton, Thomas 1776
* Trulock, Wm. 1682-1683

Watkinson, John 1684-1693

West, Thos. 1674

Wilkinson, John 1691

Williams, John 1715-1735

Williams, Mrs. Anne 1738-1744

Williams, Thos. 1738

Wilson, Richard 1730-1833

Wilson, Richard & Wm.1730-1833

Wilson, Wm. & Robert 1730-1833

Wilson & Co. 1730-1833

Wilson, Wm & Son 1730-1833

Windsop, Edward 1682

1. Rich, E.E. (Editor)—COPY BOOK OF LETTERS OUTWARD & c. 1680-1687, p. 149.
   Rich, E.E. (Editor)—MINUTES OF THE HUDSON'S BAY COMPANY 1671-1674, p. 100.
2. Thwaites, R.G.—THE JESUIT RELATIONS AND ALLIED DOCUMENTS—Vol. 43, page 65.
3. REPORT FROM SELECT COMMITTEE ON HUDSON'S BAY COMPANY, Question 5685.
4. Plenderleith, H.J.—THE CONSERVATION OF ANTIQUITIES AND WORKS OF ART, p. 192 fol.
5. Rich, E.E. (Editor)—MINUTES OF THE HUDSON'S BAY COMPANY 1671-1674, p. 84.
6. Ibid, p. 126 fn.
7. Rich, E.E. (Editor)—MINUTES OF THE HUDSON'S BAY COMPANY 1679-1682, p. 25.
8. Ibid. p. 30
9. Ibid. p. 147: Rich, E.E. (Editor)—MINUTES OF THE HUDSON'S BAY COMPANY 1682-1684, p. 31.
10. Rich, E.E. (Editor)—MINUTES OF THE HUDSON'S BAY COMPANY 1679-1682, p. 31.
11. Ibid. p. 108.
12. Ibid. p. 173, fn. 2.
13. Rich, E.E. (Editor)—MINUTES OF THE HUDSON'S BAY COMPANY 1682-1684, p. 167.
14. Hudson's Bay Archives—A 1/16 p. 12
15. Ibid. A 1/33 p. 210.
16. Ibid. A 1/35 p. 106.
17. Ibid. A 1/34 p. 236.
18. Ibid. A 1/33 p. 135.
19. Hanson Charles E.—THE NORTHWEST GUN, p. 15 fol.
20. Hudson's Bay Archives—A 26/3 p. 33.
21. Ibid. A 1/8 p. 23.

Figure 3. Flintlock found among the rocks by a small stream near the Mattagami where it runs into the Albany River, Ontario, Canada.

It is stamped with the mark of the fox as shown in Figure 2 "B".

QUANTITIES OF TRADE GUNS

The figures on the following pages are compiled from various sources.

1. The "Invoice Books" of Shipments to Hudson's Bay record the number of boxes of guns and a summary of their contents. This is the primary source for the figures on the following pages. After about 1780, the distribution problem became so complex, that it was impossible to be certain that the figures were complete. For this reason, the quantities shipped will not be given.

2. The minutes for each year usually record the quantity of guns ordered.

3. They also usually show the amount paid to the gunsmiths and occasionally this is combined with a statement of the guns received.

Sometimes all three figures agree but more often than not they disagree.

In 1714, The Committee ordered 950 guns but the shipment to Canada included only 929. Occasionally, it was necessary to estimate the number of guns purchased, basing the figure on the amount paid to the gunsmiths. This might not show in his final receipt. Nevertheless, I feel the figures are reasonably accurate. Where there has been a great discrepancy, both figures have been included.

Date	5'	4½'	4'	3½'	3'	Unk. Len.	Tot.	
1670								
1671								
1672								
1673								
1674						300	300	Ordered Mar. 24, 1674
1675								
1676								
1677								
1678						250	250	Acct. for Voyage of 1678
1679								
1680	32	32	32			42	138	Ordered 2/2/1680—42 Repaired.
1681	83	83	83			1	250	Ordered 3/21/1681
1682							450+	Oakes pattern (ordered)
1683								
1684	49	88	137	125			399	Round locks of 3 holes, etc.
1685			330	330			660	Company mark introduced.[1]
1686		41	585	636		11	1273	
1687			528	580			1108	1131 guns were paid for.
1688			52	48			100	
1689								[2](footnote)
1690		52	59	68	24		203	
1691		301	305	257	143		1006	
1692		25	400	368			793	
1693		73	328	329	3		740	7 guns were 5½ feet.
1694		60	243	187			490	
1695								
1696		5	246	350			601	20 extra guns of 4' were ordered.[3]
1697			221	231			452	Good, with bridle locks.
1698		93	204	303			600	Thumb piece, etc.
1699		103	101	101			305	
1700			300	100			400	Ordered 1/23/1700
1701			346	101			450	
1702			261				261	
1703								
1704			300				300	Ordered 1/25/1704
1705			340	110			450	
1706			150				150	
1707								
1708			300	150			450	400 guns ordered 1/30/1708
1709								
1710			200	49			249	
1711						200	200	
1712			250	131			381	
1713			202	98			300	
1714			482	173			655	Some with "white stocks".
1715			513	416			929	950 guns ordered
1716			414	288			702	
1717			755	96	36		887	

Date	5' 4½'	4'	3½'	3'	Unk. Len.	Tot.	
1718		281	450			731	
1719		150	100	50		300	
1720		251	300			551	
1721		400	60			460	
1722		326	335			661	
1723		350	148			498	
1724		271	271	33	60	635	
1725		215	290			505	
1726		200	160	100		460	
1727		201	199		100	500	
1728		125	375			500	
1729		335	290	100		725	
1730		60	251			320	
1731		590	250	150		990	
1732		320	400	80		800	
1733		245	310	180		735	
1734		150	75	85		310	
1735		75	62	13		150	
1736							
1737		375	250	25		650	
1738		275	250	25		550	650 guns ordered.
1739		275	150	150		575	675 guns ordered.
1740		375	200	25		600	Triggerguards larger than usual.
1741		275	286	164		725	
1742		250	150	100		500	
1743		225	275	125		625	
1744		200	225	100		525	
1745		300	150	75		525	
1746			125	100		225	Ordered 1/37
1747							
1748		200	150	50		400	Ordered 1/37
1749		200	200	125		525	Ordered 1/38
1750		250	150	75		475	Ordered 1/38
1751		120	125	50		295	Ordered 1/38
1752		175				175	Ordered 1/39
1753		150	125			275	Ordered 1/39
1754		375	175	25		575	Ordered 1/39
1755		175	125	25		325	Ordered 1/40
1756		250	150			400	Ordered 1/40
1757		175	100			275	Ordered 1/40
1758		175		25		200	Ordered 1/40
1759		225	50			275	Ordered 1/41
1760		225	125	50		400	Ordered 1/41
1761		300	225	75		300	
1762		450	200	75		725	24 pistols of trade.[4]
1763		375	200	75		650	
1764		150	100	30		280	
1765		50	50	75		175	
1766		91	125	58		274	"mounted as desired".[5]

Date	5′ 4½′	4′	3½′	3′	Unk. Len.	Tot.	
1767		100	115	104		319	
1768		175	185	135		495	
1769					331	331	Estimated on amount paid.
1770		225	98	50		373	
1771		250	175	25		450	
1772		288	237	154		679	5 pistols in red bags for trade.[6]
1773		172	187	134		493	
1774		150	100	50		300	
1775		125	100	75		300	
1776		206	162	25		393	
1777		175	200	50		425	
1778		290	275	160		725	
1779		75	100	25		200	
1780		47	144	46		237	
1781		156	231	81		468	

Unless otherwise noted, figures are for guns shipped.

[1] In 1685, the Company shipped 448 guns which had been made in Holland. They were ordered on Radisson's recommendations, but because of the poor quality the order was not repeated.

[2] No guns reached the Bay in 1689 because of the loss of *The Northwest Fox* and the return of the *Royal Hudson's Bay*

[3] As late as 1821, the standard H.B.C. lock did not have a bridle on the tumbler. (Chas. E. Hanson, *The Northwest Gun,* Lincoln, Nebraska 1955 p. 17)

[4] This note is not unique. Pistols were a common order but no record was made about quantities.

[5] The meaning of this note is not known, but in this period, it appears quite frequently.

[6] Supra, note 4.

Chapter 2
THE "ENGLISH PATTERN" TRADE RIFLE
by
Warren W. Caldwell

Rifled arms made for the Indian trade, as distinguished from the smoothbored fusee, commonly, the "Northwest Gun", played a significant role in national policy and in the commercial exploitation of the West. Hanson and Russell have summarized available information bearing upon the problem of the trade rifle, but despite these useful contributions, only a beginning has been made. Trade rifles are less frequent in collections than the trade gun and often are less obviously trade pieces. The "Northwest Gun" has certain specialized traits that set it off from other varieties of trade guns and distinguish it from most other contemporary firearms in common use. This is not true in the case of the trade rifle. Here, the rifle grew out of a well recognized type and even in developed form, it is often not markedly different from other contemporary arms. In particular, the "American" or "Lancaster Pattern" merely reflects the well documented transition from "Kentucky" to "Plains Rifle." While the "Northwest Gun" also underwent an evolution from its 17th Century beginnings, it was in use longer and the end product was much more distinctive than its progenitor.

Muzzle-loading rifles apparently were not in great demand in the Indian trade. The fusee was a lighter, more versatile firearm in the hands of most Indian hunters or warriors. At reasonable ranges it did the job of a rifled arm, yet it was adaptable to a greater variety of uses.

Rifles of the "Kentucky" type, and later hybridizations (The Lancaster Pattern), were produced in some quantity during the first half of the 19th century. They appear to have been widely distributed by federal "factories" as treaty rifles, and by commercial venturers. Rifled arms of the type labeled "English Pattern" were in lesser demand.[1] Hanson attributes this lack of popularity to a poorer design, relative to the more acceptable Lancaster rifles.[2] At any rate, a "New

English Pattern," incorporating new and presumably superior features of design was offered to the American Fur Company by J. Henry in 1834.[3] Published descriptions give no completely satisfactory picture of what such rifles were like but the illustration, Plate XXIVB, in Hanson[4] is probably fairly representative.

Russell states that "The development of the trade rifle paralleled that of the 'Hudson's Bay gun' in large part except that its development was strictly American."[5] This is undoubtedly true regarding the "Lancaster Pattern" but what of the English variety? The references cited above would seem to imply that the English type rifle was made only in America. Such firearms were produced by J. Henry as early as 1828.[6] If these were strictly American products, why the distinction "English Pattern"? The rifle described below if offered as an "English Pattern" trade rifle, representative of a type manufactured in England prior to the appearance of the American version. Some of the date may have been misinterpreted.

Barrel: Octagonal, 0.51 cal., 6 shallow grooves with lands of about equal width. Barrel length is 30 inches measured from the tang; diameter measures 1.0 inch across flats.

Sights: Foresight is a low fixed blade, quite wide at its base, but tapering rapidly to a knife edge. The rear sight, cut with a wide "V", is dovetailed to the barrel.

Barrel Attachment: Held to stock by three cylindrical cross-pins passing through small, loop-shaped lugs affixed to the bottom flat of the barrel.

Stock: Apparently of walnut, closely and neatly inletted for barrel and lock, "shotgun" type buttplate, cheek rest on left side.

Furniture: All of cast brass, massive and well finished; mid-portion of ramrod pipes filed to an octagonal cross section, deep annular ridges at extremities, small trigger guard with finger rest, flat angular nail plate inlet into stock, heavy buttplate with ridged cap overlapping heel of stock. Sideplate and buttplate are held in place with screws, other furniture with pins.

Trigger: Pivoting on a trigger plate inlet into stock.

Lock: Small and well made. Lockplate held to stock by two cross screws. Lower border of plate slightly convex, flat termination at rear; a deep chisel cut has upset a high ridge near rear ege of plate. Goosenecked cock, vise screw and upper jaw are replacement. Frizzen spring has small roller bearing and a tumbler bridle is present.

Markings: Birmingham proof marks, post 1813[7], die mark F A R on left flat of barrel, "Lacy and Co., London" on lockplate (in front of cock); broad arrow and letters B O stamped on right side of stock in front of buttplate.

Despite a rather poor showing in the hands of Jaeger mercenaries during the American Revolution, German muzzle-loading rifles achieved a considerable degree of popularity in late 18th Century England and bid fair to displace the more customary breech-loading stalking weapons.[8]

The "German style", as developed in England,[9] during the last quarter of the 18th Century, is obviously a close relative of its continental cousin, but with refinements. The English rifles are characteristically lighter in construction and more graceful in design. They are also of smaller caliber and of modified rifling since they were intended for deer stalking rather than for hunting of dangerous game. Like the German rifles of the period, and like others made in the Low Countries and Austria, the English examples were stocked full to the muzzle and apparently, a sliding wooden patch-box cover, a cheek rest, and set trigger were usual. The trigger guard, buttplate and other appurtenances are strongly made but less so than the continental type. The stylistic traits involved are strongly reflected in other English arms, in the "Baker Rifles", the first official rifled arms in the British service, and in the so-called "Brunswick Rifle", adopted in the 1830's.

Although it is not of first quality workmanship, the trade rifle described above is a typical example of the English-made, sporting arm in the German style. No patch box is present but details of lock work and the other indicated traits would point to a late 18th Century date. The Birmingham proof marks, however, indicate a post-1813 date of manufacture. The name "Lacy and Co., London," stamped on the lockplate, might suggest either that the lock is a replacement, or the not unknown fraud of attempting to gain the prestige of the great gun-makers of London through spurious markings. An examination of the lock inletting does not completely discount the possibility that the lock is a later addition. Very little information regarding the firm of Lacy and Company has been assembled. George[10] indicates the firm was producing firearms during the years 1803-1815; but Dr. Carlyle Smith, of the University of Kansas, has reported a lock, "obviously made for a flintlock trade gun"[11] bearing the seated fox stamp, the letters L.R. and the inscription "Lacy & Co., 1837." Glendenning[12] lists a Lacey and Company 1776, and a Lacy and Company 1880-1815. In a

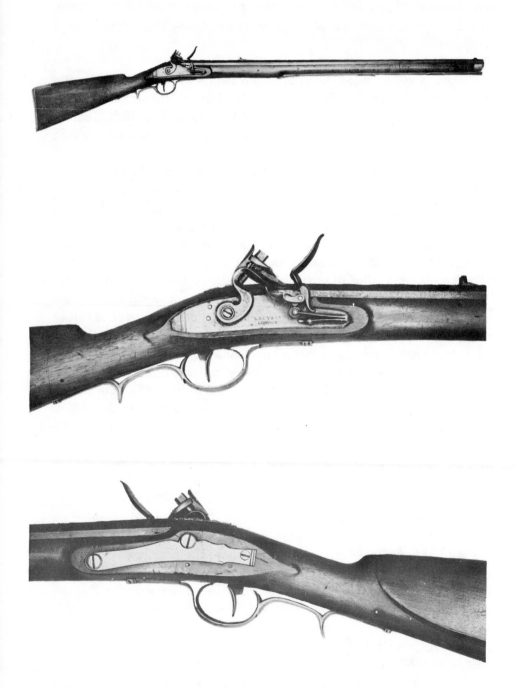

Figure 4. An English Pattern Trade Rifle.

note, he suggests that they were probably the same firm.[13] Other Lacys, in various partnerships, were in business until the 1850's. Winant[14] pictures a pepper box by Lacy and Company that must have been manufactured during this later period.

One additional example of a Lacy and Company arm that is known is a musket of typical late "Brown Bess" pattern, now in the De Young Museum, San Francisco. The musket has a percussion lock with no indication of alteration from flint ignition.

Guns marked Lacy and Company seem to have been manufactured over a considerable period so that for the moment, the trade rifle in question here cannot be dated more closely than 1813-ca.1840.

Up to this point, this rifle has been considered a trade arm without offering a detailed demonstration. Since trade rifles are not well studied, little more can be said than to offer a summary statement. The date of manufacture, as diffuse as it is, does not coincide with stylistic factors. Workmanship is plain but good. The rifle in England was a gentleman's tool; there was little or no demand for less than high quality firearms. In the same vein, the lock, whatever its status, lacks the refinements that were present in the better guns of the early 19th Century. In fact, the probable date range could place the arm well into the percussion period. Finally, the rifle closely parallels plate XXIVB in Hanson's study, specifically labeled as an "English Pattern trade rifle."[15]

The rifle has been equated to the "German Style" sporting rifles of the last quarter of the 18th Century. This, in effect, supplies a basement date for the development of the "English Pattern" rifle. The introduction into the fur trade probably began casually through purchases of rifles of plain finish but of the type already in customary manufacture for domestic use. The form must have been fairly well standardized in the trade early in the 19th Century since by 1828 (supra), they were being manufactured as a recognized pattern in America. It cannot be proven by known data that the primary manufacture of this type of rifle as a trade item began in England but the probabiliies are great that this was the case.

There is thus some basis for a suspicion that the trade rifle was not strictly an American development. Since citizens of the United States came rather late into the fur trade as large scale merchants, it is quite possible that the development of the "Lancaster Pattern" rifle was also proportionately late and that the American product was merely reflecting a degree of established demand.

Latent in this discussion, is a rather shocking idea, that is, both the

"British" and the "Lancaster" pattern rifles developed from the same progenitor. Ultimately, both are developments from the continental Jaeger, the British variant through the "German Style" rifle, the "Lancaster" through the "Kentucky" type of Pennsylvania. Each is the specialized end type product of a divergent evolution from a common ancestor.

1. Hanson (1955) THE NORTHWEST GUN, pp. 48-50.
2. ibid., p. 49.
3. Parsons (1952), "Gunmakers for the American Fur Company," NEW YORK HISTORICAL SOCIETY QUARTERLY, Vol. XXVI.
4. Hanson, op. cit., p. 80.
5. Russell, Carl P. (1957) GUNS ON THE EARLY FRONTIER, P. 130.
6. Hanson, op. cit., p. 49.
7. ibid., Figure 1, line 2, p. 56.
8. George (1947) ENGLISH GUNS AND RIFLES, p. 174.
9. ibid., Pl. XI, p.3.
10. ibid., p. 333.
11. Russell, op. cit., p. 125.
12. Glendenning (1951) BRITISH PISTOLS AND GUNS, 1640-1840, p. 180.
13. ibid., Note 43.
14. Winant (1952) PEPPERBOX FIREARMS, Figure 120, p. 115.
15. Hanson, op. cit., Pl. XXIV B, p. 80.

Chapter 3
AN INDIAN TRADE GUN OF 1680
by
Charles E. Hanson, Jr.

Early colonial flintlocks are very rare and those made purely for the Indian trade before 1700 are doubly hard to find. An intensive research program on trade guns in the Museum of the Fur Trade several years ago failed to produce any specimens which seemed thoroughly representative of the early types.

A few existing long, early muskets of .70-.85 caliber have been cited as examples of this period, but few of them have the small calibers and long, *light* barrels that contemporary descriptions and modern archaeological investigations indicate. In the 1690's the English governor of New Netherlands refused to accept heavy English muskets as gifts for the Iroquois and asked instead for the long light four and a half feet barrels from Liege. He pointed out a basic fact that was being repeated by Ramsey Crooks of the American Fur Company 150 years later: "Hunting Indians did not care to carry and use heavy guns."[1] This demand for long slender guns persisted during the next century. The Hudson's Bay Company's 1748 list of trade items included guns with four feet, three and a half feet and three feet barrels. The Jesuit relations tell that the early Dutch trade with the Mohawks was in "arquebuses." Old French sporting books illustrate the arquebus as a long, light fowling piece.

The best evidence on the character of 17th Century trade guns is of course derived from a study of archaeological specimens from old Indian village sites. Dr. Joseph Mayer made an excellent study of 17th Century gun fragments recovered from old Iroquois sites.[2] He concluded that the typical gun of that period had a barrel around fifty inches long, round or octagon at the breech, and that popular calibers were .50 to .60.

Figure 5. Early trade Arquebus from old New England Collection.
Caliber .52. Period 1680. English commercial powder horn, period 1680-1700. Horn body and brass fittings. *Photo courtesy Museum of the Fur Trade. Drawing by Charles E. Hanson, Jr.*

The frontispiece of Dr. Mayer's book is a portrait of a Mohawk chief who visited Queen Anne in 1709. The chief is holding a long, light flint musket about as tall as his jaw and fitted with a "club" or "fish-belly" stock. The barrel appears to be very slender and light at the muzzle.

Several years ago the Museum of the Fur Trade was offered a specimen from the very old Skillings collection, in Portland, Maine, that seemed to fulfill all the conditions for a typical trade gun of 1680. A drawing of this gun is in Fig. 5.

The flintlock has been repaired but it is very typical of the 1680 period with small faceted replaceable pan, a "duck-billed" hammer (round instead of pointed flint jaws) and very early frizzen. The stock could very well be American-made in "fish-belly" style and appears to be of black walnut. The barrel is most distinguished from other long Colonial muskets by its caliber. The bore now measures only .57 of an inch after a lifetime of abuse and hard service.

This barrel is thick at the breech and is octagonal for 10 5/8 inches, overall length is 45 inches and traces of the original sight remain.

The gun's furniture is also typical of the Continental fowling piece of the 1680-1700 period. The full brass buttplate has a fancy tang four inches long that suggests French influence. The rod guides are plain brass and include "tail pipe", center guide, and an upper guide that is slightly trumpet shaped. The two side-screw washers appear to be later additions to compensate for wear on the stock under the screw heads. Mayer says that screw plates did not appear until late in the 17th Century. The trigger guard is of plain brass with an engraved cross on the center of the bow. Other ornamentation includes a simple engraved band around the barrel breech, some dots and conventionalized petals on the lock, a few scrolls on the hammer and some crude line engraving on the tang of the buttplate.

The flat lockplate is 5 5/8 inches long, exactly the same as two of the three 1680 period specimens illustrated by Dr. Mayer. There is no bridle on either pan or tumbler. The frizzen spring is found to be externally attached.

There is no trigger plate, the barrel is attached by three pins and by a tang screw coming up from below to screw into the barrel tang. There are no proof-marks or stampings on the gun except for a now indecipherable name in script on the top flat of the barrel. The last three letters in the name are "—ard". In overall general appearance the gun resembles an example of the 1660-1680 period illustrated in Pollard's HISTORY OF FIREARMS.[3]

It could have been manufactured in England or France, but the strongest possibility is that at least the basic parts were imported from Holland. At any rate it is believed to be a good example of the type which found popularity with the Indians of early colonial days. It is certainly too light and carries too small a charge to have done service as a militia musket or even as a settler's all-purpose musket.

An interesting sidelight on the acquisition of this Colonial musket is an early horn powder flask from New England which was given to the museum twenty-eight years ago. (Fig. 5) It is a very representative example of the flasks being made and sold in England in the 1680 period.[4] The measuring neck and the base cap are made of brass—the usual material for those fittings after 1670 (earlier English flasks are mounted in iron). The original owner of the 1680 trade gun may well have purchased and carried a flask very similar to this one.

1. Crooks in letter to J. Henry in 1840.
2. Mayer, Joseph R. FLINTLOCKS OF THE IROQUOIS, 1620-1687 (Rochester, New York; Rochester Museum of Arts and Science, 1943).
3. Pollard, Hugh Bennet C., A HISTORY OF FIREARMS, (1926), London.
4. Glendenning, Ian. BRITISH PISTOLS AND GUNS, 1640-1840 (Cassell and Co., Ltd. London, 1950, pp. 14-16.)

Chapter 4
THE GUNSMITH'S CACHE FROM MALTA BEND, MISSOURI
by
T.M. Hamilton

In the fall of 1933, a fifteen year old boy named Joe LeFaivre discovered a cache consisting of 108 gun parts, eighteen gunsmithing tools, six unidentified objects of iron, and the lock of an old chest. There can be no question that this find represents the stock and tools of an old frontier gunsmith who buried his equipment in a wooden chest and never got back to reclaim his property.*

From conversations with the individuals who were present when Joe made his discovery it seems that certain parts, which Joe instantly recognized as flintlocks, were found by him north of Malta Bend, Missouri, in the center of a freshly graded road. Mr. Wheeler Huff and Mr. Maurice Pollard, both of Marshall, Missouri, upon being shown the find by Joe, ran around the spot with the grader while he and a friend of his, Howard Williams, dug up the road and the side ditch for any remaining parts.

The cache was made at a spot where the ground rises slightly above the general level of the surrounding prairie and approximately 1,000 yards south of the eastern edge of the Little Osage village upon which there is a tentative date of 1730-1775 from documentary references. Carl Chapman, who has made an intensive study of Osage history, states that the tentative termination date can be considered to be within five years of the actual one, since the Little Osage had left Saline County, Missouri, by 1780.

---

*Today this Gunsmith's Cache is part of an outstanding collection of archaeological surface materials and it has been placed with the University of Missouri as a memorial to Joe LeFaivre by his parents, Mr. and Mrs. A.C. LeFaivre, and can be seen in the Museum of Anthropology in Columbia, Missouri.

Because of the proximity of the cache to the village it is natural to assume that there was some connection between the two. If it can be shown from an examination of its contents that the materials in the cache were contemporary with those of the village, then this connection can be considered as established since the village was a permanent one.

It should be mentioned here that the history of this village site is complicated. Because of the old spring at the foot of the bluff, it was a favorite stopping place for the early traders who pioneered and established the Santa Fe Trail. There is also the possibility that the site was occupied overnight by occasional fur trading expeditions during the intervening years or from about 1780 to 1820. However, these occupations could have left little evidence because they were relatively small and infrequent.

It is known from Garrard[1] and others that the Northwest Gun was a favorite arm of the Canadian ox-skinners and other *engages* on the Santa Fe Trail as late as the 1840's, so the presence of serpent sideplates, oxbow trigger guards, and other characteristic parts of that gun on the site of the Little Osage village itself does not necessarily mean that they were left there by the Osage. Also, shortly after 1820, the first percussion guns began making their appearance and since most of the Santa Fe traders themselves were men of substance and would be prone to adopt the improved ignition system, it is reasonable to assume that percussion gun parts found on the site are the result of that activity or later.

All of the items from the cache itself are badly rusted and deeply pocked. The combination of soil and climate in this section of Missouri seems to be peculiarly effective in promoting rust on iron objects. From correspondence with S. James Gooding and Moreau S. Maxwell it is obvious that lockplates found in Canada and Michilimackinac have suffered far less injury from prolonged exposure than those in this area of Missouri. So far, no lettering nor proofmarks have been found, but experience with the lockplates from the Osage sites in Vernon County, Missouri, indicates that five or, possibly, six of them might yield markings if properly cleaned and etched. However, the authorities have been understandably reluctant to permit anything other than visual inspection.

Here is a unique find which, if interpreted properly, would give a rare insight into both the operations of the itinerant gunsmith and his sources of supply.

Figure 6. Tools from the Gunsmith's Cache.
Top: A hand vise used in holding small objects.
Middle: A mainspring vise for placing or removing the mainspring.
Bottom: A half round metal file, broken.

Figure 7. Tools from the Gunsmith's Cache.
From top to bottom: The upper item is a saw made by filing teeth in the blade of a case knife. Below it is the remains of a drawknife, probably used in shaping a gunstock. A screwdriver for sidescrews is immediately below the drawknife. The blades of three straight and two offset gouges are below the screwdriver. The gouges were used in inletting gunstocks.

For instance, it is believed that the gunsmith took these parts from discarded guns, because no complete guns or assembled locks are found on village sites. True, lockplates are found with some parts, but they almost always show signs of systematic stripping—either by the Indians themselves, or by the gunsmiths. It can only be concluded that the parts were being removed from the locks with the ultimate purpose of repairing other guns and that these particular items in the cache were also salvaged from guns which had outlived their usefulness.

As a first step in identification, the lockplates and cocks were photographed and sets of prints sent various authorities to see if there might be some unanimity of opinion. There was general agreement as to the date of manufacture of some of the gun parts, but all were very reluctant to say where any particular piece was manufactured. For instance, Mr. A.N. Kennard of H.M. Tower of London[2] states that lock No. 21 (Fig. 13, p. 43) was "of English type circa 1720-40" and that the cocks type Nos. 1 and 2 (Fig. 17, p. 47) were "typically English of late eighteenth century type, i.e., flat with chamfered edges and rather sharply curved necks." At no place did he, or any of the other authorities consulted, state flatly that a given gun part was of either French or English origin.

Working within the limits of our present knowledge it is thought that the cache was made sometime between 1770-1780. Since the presence of the chest lock indicates that the gun parts and tools were buried in a wooden box, it is possible the gunsmith was a white man rather than an Indian. The flint locks are somewhat large for rifles of that period, but are characteristic of those used on smoothbores. Also, there are no other items in the cache characteristic of a rifle. Unless this gunsmith was traveling with a trader when the cache was made—in which event he would surely be carrying some rifle parts for the party—the only other reason for his being in that particular neighborhood during that period would be because the Osage were his customers. Therefore, the probabilities are that he made the cache while the Little Osage village was still occupied.

Little else can be said at this time about the materials from this cache. The tabulation of dimensions from the lockplates (p. 37) may be of assistance later in identifying some of them when used in conjunction with the photographs, (pp. 38-46).

The cocks are grouped in the illustrations as closely as possible by type. The remaining cocks were examined and marked at a different time. This happened since it was not practical to have all of the gun

33

parts out of the case for extended periods of time. There was a total of 34 locks found in the Gunsmith's Cache.

In the captions accompanying the illustrations of the lockplates, dates or origin have not been assigned because knowledge at this time is too vague and confused except in a few isolated instances. For instance, Mr. Kennard's tentative identification of Lock No. 21 (Fig. 13, p.43) will probably stand, but that lock is distinguished by being the only one upon which there seems to be any agreement whatever among the authorities who have examined the photographs from the find.

The single fusil barrel, not pictured here, may eventually prove to be an important item in unraveling the early history of the fur trade. That it has a broken tang is not particularly surprising, but why should it be hammered down against the breech plug? Apparently it had been used as a peg before coming into the gunsmith's possession. It may well be that he could not afford to be too particular about his sources of supply.

The important features about this barrel are its dimensions. The bore is approximately .41 caliber and it measures 1-1/32 inches cross the flats at the breech. This is by far the smallest bore so far found in an Indian trade gun; and, as with the Osage guns of .44 caliber it probably came from a gun of early 18th Century French manufacture.

Lockplates with unbridled tumbler	5
Lockplates with bridled tumbler	3
Lockplates without tumblers	26
Total lockplates	34
Cocks, type No. 1	3
Cocks, type No. 2	6
Cocks, type No. 3	1
Cocks, type No. 4	4
Cocks, type No. 5	6
Cocks, type No. 6	8
Cocks, type No. ?	2
Cocks on locks	4
Total cocks	34
Mainsprings	9
Frizzen springs	3
Sidescrews	3
Flint vise screws	4
Frizzens	13
Sears	1
Trigger plates	2
Trigger with trigger plate	1
Fusil barrel (Now 16 inches long. Tang broken and hammered against breech plug.)	1
Ramrod pipe, front	1
Ramrod pipe, rear for fullstock gun	1
Trigger guard (Definitely not Northwest Gun type.)	1
Total number of gun parts	108

GUNSMITHING TOOLS

Handvise	1
Mainspring vise	1
Metal file, half round, broken	1
Wood rasp, half round, 12½ inches long	1

Wood saw made from knife blade		1
Drawknives		2
Screwdriver		1
Case knives		2
Inletting tools—Straight gouges		3
Offset gouges		2
Wedges (old broken axe blades)		2
Heavy hammer head, broken in eye		1
Total gunsmithing tools		18
Lock on tool chest		1
Unidentified objects of iron		6
GRAND TOTAL		133

TABULATON OF LOCKS AND LOCKPLATES
FROM THE GUNSMITH'S CACHE

No attempt has been made to force plates into preconceived length groupings; measurements are made, regardless of present condition of plates, to within closest 1/32nd of an inch.

No lockplates have bridled frizzens. Locks No. 4, 8 and 22 have bridled tumblers. Locks No. 1, 2, 21, 23 and 27 do not.

Under Pan: s=pan separable from plate; i=pan integral with plate; r=pan definitely rounded; v=pan definitely "V"; f=flat and modified either r or v.

Under Frizzen Spring Screw: h = hidden screw; e = exposed screw.

Lock or Lock plate	Pan		Lock plate Length	Width	Frizzen Spring Screw	Ledge Length
1	i?	v	5-3/8	1-1/16	e?	2-5/16
2	s?	fv	5-3/8	1-1/16	h	2
3	s	fv	5-7/16	1-1/16	e	2-1/8
4	s	fv	5-15/32	1	h	2-5/16
5	s	fv?	5-1/2	1-1/16	e	2-1/32
6	s	?	5-1/2	1-1/16	e	?
7	s	fv	5-1/2	1-1/16	h	2-7/16
8	s	v	5-3/8	1	h	2-3/8
9	s	?	5-1/2	1-1/16	h	?
10	s	fv	5-7/16	1-1/32	h	1-15/16

Lock or Lock plate	Pan		Lock plate Length	Width	Frizzen Spring Screw	Ledge Length
11	s	fr	5-9/16	1-1/16	e	1-13/16
12	s?	r	5-7/16	1-1/32	h	1-7/8
13	s	v?	5-17/32	1-1/16	h	1-15/16
14	s	fv	5-9/16	1-1/16	h	2-1/16
15	s	?	5-11/16	1-3/32	h	?
16	s	fv	5-1/2	1-1/16	h	2-7/16
17	s	r	5-19/32	1-3/32	h?	1-7/8
18	i?	v?	5-19/32	1-3/32	h	2-1/2
19	s?	fv?	5-17/32	1-3/32	h	2
20	s	fv	5-3/4	1-1/16	h	2
21	s	r	5-7/16	1-1/32	e?	2
22	s	?	5-5/8	1	h	?
23	s	v	5-5/8	1-1/16	e	2-1/4
24	s	r?	5-27/32	1-1/8	h	2-1/2
25	i?	fv	6	1-1/8	e	2-7/16
26	s	r	5-3/4	1-1/16	h	2
27	i	r?	5-3/4	1-1/4	e?	2-25/32
28	s	fv	5-3/4	1-1/8	h	2-9/16
29	s?	fv	5-5/8	1-1/16	h	2-1/2
30	s	fv	5-5/8	1-1/16	h	1-7/8
31	s	v	6-5/32	1-3/16	e	2-13/16
32	s	r	6-3/32	1-1/16	e	1-5/8
33	i	v?	6-3/8	1-5/32	e	2-5/16
34	s	r?	6	1-1/8	h	2-1/4

Figure 8. Locks No. 1 to No. 4 from the Gunsmith's Cache.

Figure 9. Locks No. 5 to No. 8 from the Gunsmith's Cache.

Figure 10. Locks No. 9 to No. 12 from the Gunsmith's Cache.

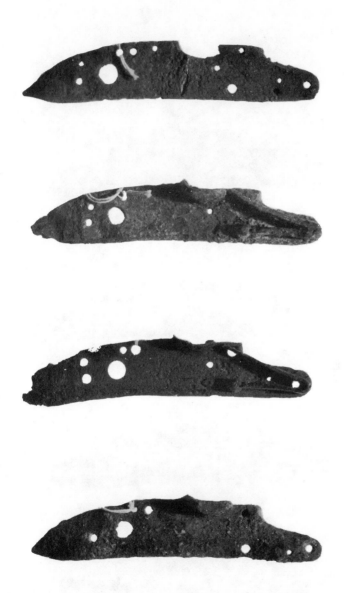

Figure 11. Locks No. 13 to No. 16 from the Gunsmith's Cache.

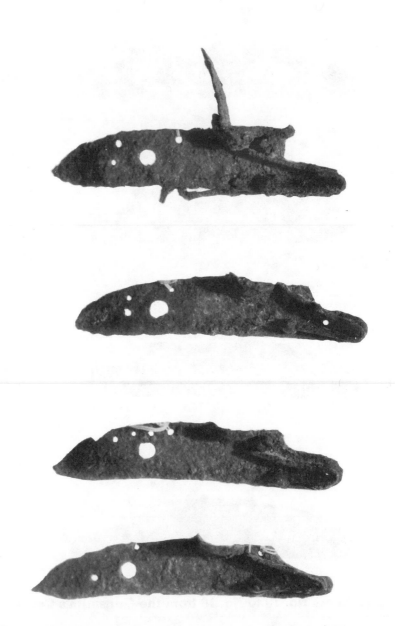

Figure 12. Locks No. 17 to No. 20 from the Gunsmith's Cache.

Figure 13. Locks No. 21 to No. 24 from the Gunsmith's Cache.

Figure 14. Locks No. 25 to No. 28 from the Gunsmith's Cache.

Figure 15. Locks No. 29 to No. 32 from the Gunsmith's Cache.

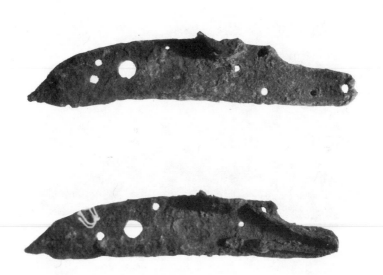

Figure 16. Locks No. 33 and No. 34 from the Gunsmith's Cache.

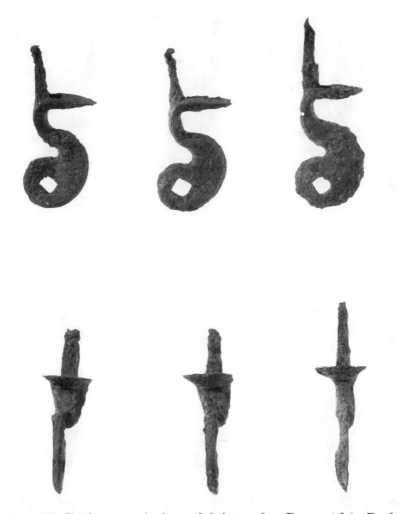

Figure 17. Cocks type 1, 2, and 3 from the Gunsmith's Cache.
Types No. 1 and No. 2 are typical of the English form of the late 18th Century with flat
bases, chamfered edges, sharply curved necks and narrow combs. Though type 3 also
has a narrow comb, note that it has a "step" on the front face of the comb which acted
as a fulcrum for the upper jaw of the flint vise. The base of this cock is rounded. Type
No. 3 is typical of the English cocks of the early 18th Century.

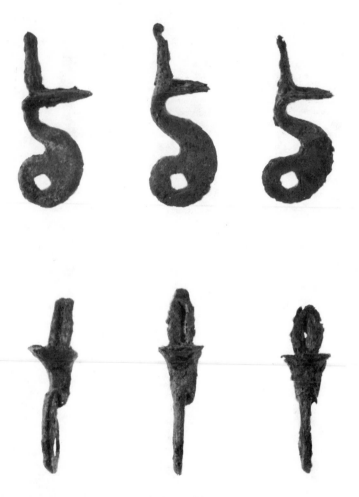

Figure 18. Cocks type 4, 5, and 6 from the Gunsmith's Cache.
In general, cocks with a groove in the center of a wide comb had their greatest
popularity during the middle of the 18th Century. These cocks could be English,
French, or from the low countries of Europe.

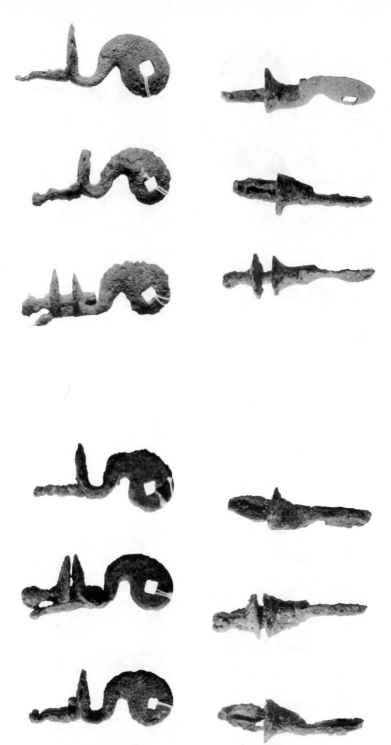

Figure 19. Cocks from the Gunsmith's Cache.

Figure 20. Cocks from the Gunsmith's Cache.

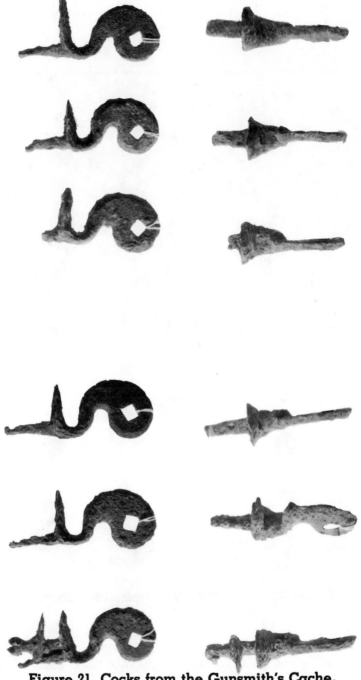

Figure 21. Cocks from the Gunsmith's Cache.

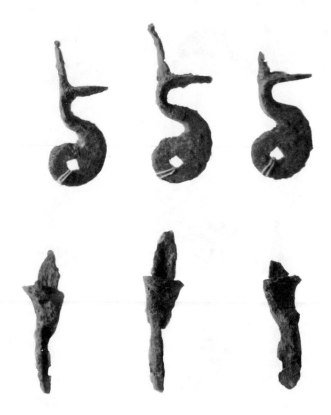

Figure 22. Cocks from the Gunsmith's Cache.

1. Garrard, Lewis H. (1955) WAH-TO-YAH AND THE TAOS TRAIL, Norman, Oklahoma.
2. Kennard, A.N. Sept. 26, 1958, Personal Letter.

Chapter 5
RELICS FROM 17th CENTURY SENECA SITES
by
T.M. Hamilton

Joseph R. Mayer gives an excellent review of the Indian and the trade gun during the 17th Century.[1] The following comments, dealing particularly with the Seneca, are based upon information furnished in correspondence with Charles F. Wray of West Rush, New York, Harry L. Schoff of Holcomb, New York and John Witthoft, who in 1960 was Chief Curator of the Pennsylvania State Museum.

It seems that very little data on firearms in the Indian trade during the initial stages of contact on the Eastern seaboard is available. There are parts of a wheellock gun now in the United States National Museum found at the Indian site of Kikotan. A Susquehannock village in Lancaster County, Pennsylvania, known as the Washingtonboro site, having an occupational date of 1600-1620, has furnished only one lead ball of .40 caliber, some swan shot, but no gun parts in spite of rather extensive excavating. Mr. Witthoft felt that this could be safely considered the initial introduction of the gun into Indian hands in this area of the United States.[2]

Wray and Schoff provide the location and occupational periods of the various post contact villages until the time of DeNonville's raid in 1687. They find that the "Seneca had two coexisting great villages which moved seven times in approximately 150 years in a general northward direction". These village sites are all within an area of about 100 square miles in the present state of New York; in the counties of Monroe, Ontario and Livingston, to be exact. The two earliest historic sites of these co-existing great villages, known as Adams and Tram, were fortified and occupied hill tops approximately one-half mile apart![3]

The names of the series of sites and the periods of occupation, as worked out by Wray and Schoff, are as follows:

OCCUPATIONAL PERIOD	VILLAGE GROUPS No. 1	No. 2
1550-1575	Adams	Tram
1575-1590	Cameron	

Figure 23. A complete gun, with barrel, lock, trigger, and trigger guard from grave at Rochester Junction Site.

From the Harry L. Schoff collection. Photo courtesy Mr. Schoff.

1590-1615	Dutch Hollow	Factory Hollow
	Feugie	Vita-Taft
		Conn
1616-1630	Lima	Warren
	Bosleyes Mills	
1630-1650	Power House	Steele
1650-1675	Dann	Marsh
		Fox
1675-1687	Rochester Junction	Boughton Hill
	Kirkwood	Fort
		Beal
		Bunce

Glass cane beads are the first articles of European manufacture to appear, being found at both Adams and Tram. It was not until the Power House and Steele sites were occupied in about 1630 that gun parts are found. The snaphaunce was popular at those two places, but had practically disappeared by the time the Seneca moved to the Dann and Marsh sites some 20 years later. The doglock is even more prevalent at Power House and Steele than the snaphaunce, and continues through the early occupation of Rochester Junction and Boughton Hill. On the other hand, the true flintlock is found sparingly at Power House and Steele, but by the beginning of occupation of the Dann and Marsh sites in about 1650, it is the dominating firearm.[4]

If nothing else, the foregoing indicates how exacting a time indicator gun parts can be once we have the various types properly identified and described.

It is interesting to note in passing that Wray and Schoff conclude that most of the Seneca graves were robbed soon after burial of all "useful items such as wampum, glass beads, iron axes, and good brass kettles", while the ordinary native material was left behind. As the early white settlers began to infiltrate the country, the graves were again ransacked; "This time the scavengers were in quest of iron for the blacksmiths . . .".[5]

Mr. Schoff advances an interesting theory on the first and most important use to which the Indian put the gun. He noticed that there were a large number of detached gunlocks found in the earlier post-contact Seneca graves, and that the flint and steel strike-a-light, which quickly became a popular trade item with the natives, was seldom found in a grave which had one of these gunlocks. Since gunpowder was undoubtedly difficult to procure and even more difficult to keep dry without proper flasks during the early introductory years of the trade,

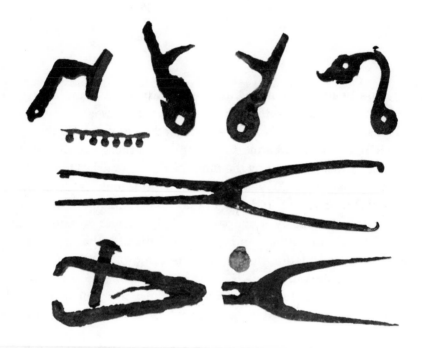

Figure 24. Boughton Hill Site Gun Parts.

From left to right: Battery from a snaphaunce, cock from an early dog lock, a mid-17th Century type cock, and the serpentine from a matchlock. A strip of swanshot still attached to the sprue and a six-shot mould for swanshot.

Lower row: A hand vise for filing tumblers and sears, a .65 caliber bullet, and a bullet mold.

Harry L. Schoff collection. Photo courtesy Mr. Schoff.

Mr. Schoff concluded that, at first, the Indian valued the gun primarily as a fire maker rather than as a weapon. Later, when the traders became more common and competition more keen, the Indians were able to get good powder and powder flasks, and the gun became an everyday tool and eventually supplanted the bow.[6]

Mr. Witthoft seems to agree in general with Wray and Schoff on the sequence of occupation, but appparently assigns somewhat earlier dates to developments in acculturation. For instance, Wray states that brass arrowheads first made their appearance between 1600 and 1620 and are common until 1700, while flint arrowheads are seldom found on Seneca sites after 1650.[7] Witthoft is of the opinion that practically no arrowheads of either flint or brass are found on Seneca or Susquehannock sites after 1640.[8] In either event, it appears as if the bow was quickly demoted to a minor place in the Indian economy.

In this same letter, Witthoft points out that there was an abrupt break in the beaver market in 1675. As a consequence, the Indians could buy comparatively few guns thereafter, and took far better care of them than they had during the boom years of the early fur trade. During those lush times, guns had been used lavishly as grave offerings, but after 1675 there was a marked tendency to keep the guns for the use of the living. Apparently, the Seneca never again could afford such spendthrift ways as they had experienced during the middle years of the 17th Century.[9]

The following inventories of gun parts and associated materials are from burials at two different Seneca village sites excavated by Albert J. Hoffman of Holcomb, New York.

From the Marsh site:

Gunlocks	1
Lockplates. One with mainspring.	2
Cocks.	3
Frizzens.	5
Flashpans.	2
Tumblers.	6
Mainsprings.	3
Lock screws.	5
Screws.	4
Ramrod pipes.	4

Gun tools:
Pincers.	1
Whetstone.	1
Iron knife.	1
Small section lead	1
Bear Tusks.	2
Wolf tusks,	2
Stone celt.	1

From Marsh site:
Gunlocks. Three with flints.	7
Lockplates. Two with springs, three with pans.	5
Cocks.	5
Mainsprings.	6
Frizzen springs.	3
Triggers.	3
Lock screws.	2
Upper jaws.	4
Buttplates, iron.	1
Gun flints.	4
Bullet molds.	1
Iron knives.	4
Iron axe blade sections.	4
Iron ring.	1
Iron fishhook (?)	1
Whetstones.	3

From Boughton Hill:
Gunlocks complete with flints.	2
Lockplates complete with pans.	7
Lockplates with mainsprings.	2
Lockplates.	8
Sideplate, brass.	1
Trigger guard.	1
Sear springs.	3
Small axes or chisels made from gun parts.	4
Section of lead.	1
Axe Blade.	1

If there is any one peculiarity concerning these Seneca burials it is the great number of individual parts belonging to the gunlocks. Mayer mentions that Schoff recovered 426 flintlock parts in one mass from a burial at Boughton Hill.[10] Schoff also found 151 parts plus two complete locks in burial No. 177 at the Marsh site, also known as St. Michaels or the Mud Creek site. He further states that he has "uncovered a large number of small caches consisting of from two or three to fifteen or twenty miscellaneous parts which were individual grave offerings", and that there are a total of "three large caches where the parts numbered more than 100".[11] Since DeNonville's raid terminated the occupation of Boughton Hill in 1687, it seems most likely that the burials were made during the flush years immediately preceding the break in the beaver market in 1675. Mayer suggests that the hoard of 426 lock parts represents the stock of a native dealer which were buried with him, and the evidence seems to bear him out.[12]

Figure 25. Tools from Seneca Burials.

Schoff advances the theory that these hoards of gunlock parts had been stripped from old lockplates and were being traded among the Indians as repair parts.[13] No other reason for accumulating such stocks of parts seems reasonable.

The interesting thing is that Schoff succeeded in building two functioning flintlocks from the parts found at Boughton Hill, which indicates that the parts could not have been too badly worn at the time of their accumulation and that also, these parts were manufactured to much closer tolerances than we have hitherto assumed. Since Eli Whitney is credited with being the first manufacturer to introduce true interchangability of parts by maintaining close tolerances in the machining operations, this achievement of the Dutch, some 200 years earlier, deserved to be recognized. Here is Schoff's reply to a specific inquiry concerning the assembly of the two locks:

"By sorting the parts I was able to assemble two locks that would work. I cleaned up the parts on a wire brush wheel and assembled them with only minor fitting. It must be remembered, however, that these parts were from the same cache and could have conceivably been from the same lock. This I doubt as there were many more parts than lock plates to accommodate them and would appear this was a repairman's stock in trade simply gathered from the village litter where discarded by their Indian owners after breakage or lack of powder."[14]

Within less than fifty years after the introduction of the gun, the Indians were apparently carrying on a lively trade among themselves in repair parts. The popular conception that the Indians were overwhelmed with the mysteries of the firearm, is further undermined by the evidence of the gunsmithing tools also found on same sites. Fig. 25 shows a drawknife and a knife with a curved blade, both of which were standard tools used in restocking guns. The drawknife roughed out the stock, while the knife with the curved blade was used to inlet the lock. In the same photograph is shown a three cornered file of the type used to file sears and tumblers. The handvise shown in Fig. 24, p. 56 could only be of use to someone engaged in locksmithing, or equally exacting work, where it was necessary to hold small objects to be filed or otherwise fitted within a mechanism. The evidence indicates that the natives quickly acquired an understanding of the mechanics of the gun certainly equal to that of the average white backwoodsman.

From the information available at this time it seems that these 17th Century guns, initially used in the Indian trade, were primarily of the large bores which characterized the military weapons of that day. Schoff, upon rechecking, reports that he has in his collection balls ranging from .400 inches in diameter to .750 inches with most of them

Figure 26. Locks from various Seneca Sites of the 17th Century.
Upper: A snaphaunce from the Power House site, period 1630-1650. The lock measures 8 1/8 inch long from extreme left end to end of battery spring.
Second row: Flint lock from Rochester Junction site, 1675-1687. A flintlock from the Dann site, period 1650-1675.
Bottom row: Two locks from the Boughton Hill site, 1675-1687.
From the Harry L. Schoff collection. Photo courtesy Mr. Schoff.

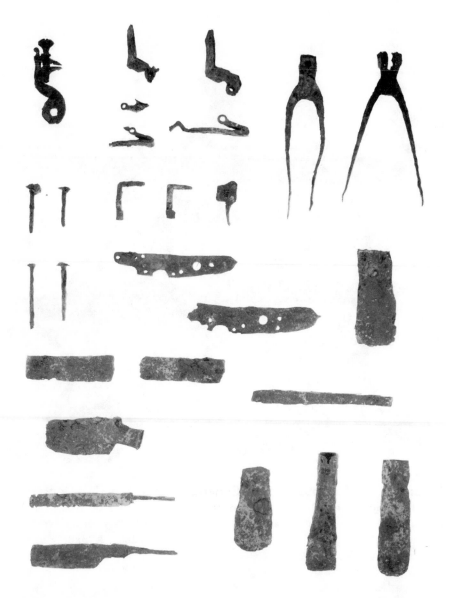

Figure 27. Gun parts and gun tools from a burial on the Beal Farm, Victor, New York.

This site dates approximately from 1675-1687.

From the Charles F. Wray collection. Photo courtesy Rochester Museum of Arts and Sciences.

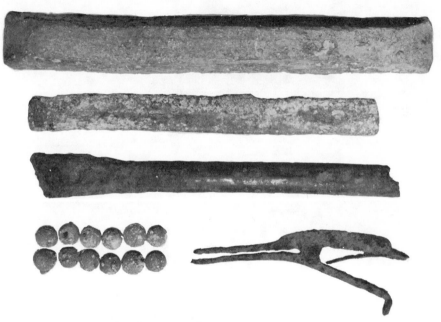

Figure 28. Bullet making items.
First two items at top are bars of lead for making bullets. The third item is a flattened
musket barrel. Below are twelve lead bullets of .65 caliber and a pair of tongs for picking up burning embers [Smokers' Companion].
From the Harry L. Schoff collection. Photo courtesy Mr. Schoff.

Figure 29. Parts of a flintlock pistol found at the Dann site, Honeoye Falls, New York, period 1650-1675.

From the Charles F. Wray collection. Photo courtesy Rochester Museum of Arts Sciences.

Figure 30. Gun parts from the Marsh site.
Springs, lock parts, European flints and two brass trigger guards from a cache found
in grave No. 177.
From the Harry L. Schoff collection. Photo courtesy Mr. Schoff.

Figure 31. Component parts of 17th Century flintlock selected from cache described by Mayer in FLINTLOCKS OF THE IROQUOIS.

1. Vise screw. 2. Cock. 3. Upper vise jaw. 4. Flint. 5. Lockplate. 6. Pan. 7. Frizzen, battery or hammer. 8. Frizzen spring. 9. Frizzen screw. 10. Frizzen spring screw. 11. Mainspring. 12. Mainspring screw. 13. Tumbler screw. 14. Tumbler. 15. Sear screw. 16. Sear. 17. Sear spring. Period 1650-1670.

From the Harry L. Schoff collection. Photo courtesy Mr. Schoff.

Figure 32. An antique tinderlighter of the 17th Century shown with the remains of one of similar construction. From grave at Rochester Junction site.

From the Harry L. Schoff collection. Photo courtesy Mr. Schoff.

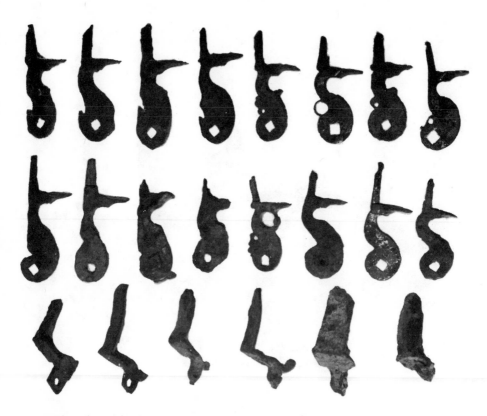

Figure 33. Cocks and Frizzens from Seneca sites.

The first four cocks on top row are from dog locks. The remaining four cocks have small rings in back, as does the fifth cock in second row.

The first four cocks in second row are of the straight type, while the last three are late 17th Century types.

The bottom row illustrates frizzens from caches.

From the Harry L. Schoff collection. Photo courtesy Mr. Schoff.

Figure 34. Gun parts in the Charles F. Wray collection.
A dog lock with dog still engaging cock. Two side screws, a trigger and a trigger guard are shown above the lock. The object in upper right hand corner is unidentified.

Photo courtesy Rochester Museum of Arts and Sciences.

falling in the .575 to .625 inch diameter group. Those under .500 are rare and he thinks that they were probably used as buckshot rather than balls.[15] The .40 caliber ball, mentioned by Witthoft, from the Washingtonboro site, and having an occupational date of 1600-1620, could also have been a buckshot and not a bullet. It is interesting to note that most of the balls shown in these illustrations seem to be .65 caliber.

From correspondence it is evident that there is a tremendous amount of gun material from sites of the early contact period in the East. It seems there is some evidence that rifles were also introduced into the trade at this time[16] but the extent of this introduction has not been defined. The presence of pistols is to be expected, but brass barreled blunderbusses were another surprising innovation.

1. Mayer, Jos. R (1943) FLINTLOCKS OF THE IROQUOIS.
2. Witthoft, John (1958) Personal Letter, Sept. 20.
3. Wray, Chas. F. and Schoff, Harry L. (1953) PRELIMINARY REPORT ON THE SENECA SEQUENCE IN WESTERN NEW YORK, 1550-1687.
4. ibid.
5. ibid.
6. Schoff, Harry L. (1957) Personal Letter, Dec. 3.
7. Wray, Chas. F. (1957) Personal Letter, Dec. 26.
8. Witthoft, op. cit.
9. ibid.
10. Mayer, op. cit., pp. 32-33.
11. Schoff, (1958), Personal letter, Mar. 13.
12. Mayer, op. cit., p. 33.
13. Schoff, (1959), Personal letter, Apr. 1.
14. ibid.
15. Schoff, (1960), Personal letter, June 1.
16. Witthoft, op. cit.

Chapter 6
RELICS FROM 18th CENTURY OSAGE SITES
by
T.M. Hamilton

There are three important collections of 18th Century gun parts, associated with Osage Indian village sites. They are the Malta Bend Gunsmith's Cache, discovered during the early 1930's by Joe LeFaivre, the J.M. Crick collection, Corder, Missouri, and the material in the Department of Anthropology, University of Missouri. This chapter will confine itself to the last two collections.

There is reason to believe that there were five individual Osage Indian villages within the confines of the present State of Missouri during historic times.[1] Some of these sites may have been occupied either before or after the dates shown in the following tabulation, since they are merely the chance recordings found among the papers of our early explorers and traders. All that is certain is that these sites were occupied during the periods shown.

THE SITE NUMBERS ARE KEYS OF LOCATION FOR THE FOLLOWING TEXT INFORMATION.

SITE NUMBER	VICINITY	COUNTY	TRIBE	TENTATIVE DATES
Unlocated	--	Saline	Little Osage	1714-1724
23Sa3	Malta Bend	Saline	Little Osage	1730-1775
23Ve4	Nevada	Vernon	Little Osage	1775-1815
23Ve3	Nevada	Vernon	Big Osage	—1775—
23Ve1	Nevada	Vernon	Big Osage	1790-1815

Phil E. Chappell shows a sketch of the site, now known as 23Sa3 near Malta Bend, as it appeared in 1902. Apparently,the ground had been cleared a few years previously and he states that "Mr. J.S. Tobin, a reliable gentleman, who has lived near the locality for many years, says that he believes that more than a hundred gun barrels have been unearthed."[2] Chappell makes no mention of gunlocks or other gun furniture.

Twelve years later, Ed C. Hill in writing of the same site also estimates that "no less than one hundred gun barrels have been car-

Figure 35

INVENTORY OF GUN PARTS FROM FOUR OSAGE VILLAGE SITES

SITE	1730-1775 23Sa3	1775-1815 23Ve4	-1775 23Ve3	1790-1815 23Vel
Locks	1	0	0	0
Lockplates	10	3	6	23
Cocks	3	3	3	6
Frizzens	5	0	2	3
Buttplates, iron	1	0	1	0
Buttplates, brass	11	0	1	13
Trigger guards, iron	6	0	1	0
Trigger guards, brass	8	0	3	8
Sideplates, serpent, flat brass	0	0	0	3
Sideplates, serpent, cast brass	1	0	1	8
Sideplates, iron	2	0	0	0
Sideplates, brass	1	0	0	0
Ramrod pipes, brass	2	0	0	0
Ramrod pipes, iron	2	0	0	0
Mainsprings, gun	3	0	2	4
Mainsprings, pistol	1	0	0	0
Triggers	2	1	0	2
Trigger plates	1	0	1	2
Flint screws	1	0	0	0
Tumblers	0	0	1	0
Tumblers bridles	1	0	0	0
Sears	0	1	1	0
Frizzen springs	0	0	0	1
Flint vise caps	0	0	1	1
Inlays	0	0	0	1
Barrel fragments	33	4	19	171
Bullets	16	0	2	0
Bullets made into beads	1	0	0	0
Breech plugs	5	0	2	1
Gun flints				
Native	95	1	33	28
French		0	13	4
English		4	1	21
Gunsmithing tools				
Handvise	0	0	0	1
Flat files	0	1	1	1
Half round files	0	0	1	0
Three cornered files	0	0	0	1
Gouge or screwdriver	0	0	1	1

ried away." He concludes, quite naturally, that, because the gun barrels "show conclusively that they have been broken by violence", that the site had been the scene of a "massacre," and wonders why the victors deliberately destroyed such valuable property. Hill also concludes that there must have been a gun shop present since some breech sections had been found with the breech plugs removed. He reports the finding of only one lock, but it is a very important find for us in this study since the French name of the maker, "Thielliers Freres" could still be made out.[3]

Both Chappell and Hill were conservative in their estimate of the number of gun barrels found and removed from 23Sa3. The 209 barrel fragments listed in the inventories shown in this report can be but a fraction of the total number removed from these sites in the past and now lost.

By far the major number of gun parts from 23Sa3 is in the Crick collection; that of the University of Missouri being but a few barrel fragments. See Fig. 35 for comparative inventories.

The Little Osage probably moved from Saline County to Vernon County in 1775, but this date may be off one way or the other by a few years (Chapman, personal comment). The site of this new village (23Ve4) has been almost completely obliterated by coal mining operations, so very little material has been recovered by the University of Missouri.[4]

Just when the Big Osage first occupied their village now known as 23Ve3 is unknown. However, there is one possible documentary reference to it in 1775.[5] This village probably moved as a unit to 23Ve1 about 1790.

Discussions of the material from the four known Osage villages will be by parts rather than by sites, since it is difficult to point out variations in parts manufacture when all types from all sites are not under consideration at the same time. Conclusions will be reached as to which types properly belong to a given period—whether early, middle, or late 18th Century—and also differentiate, when possible, between parts of French and English manufacture. In doing this, it must be taken into consideration the many uncertainties resulting from (1) the variations in manufacture, even within the same gunsmith's shop, which charaterizes hand craft, and (2) the time lag between the introduction of new designs in Europe and their arrival on the frontier. Both of these factors are at present recognized but largely unknown.

Figure 36. Gun barrel fragments from Little Osage site 23Sa3.

GUN BARRELS

There is a total of 227 gun barrel sections from the four Osage sites. Without exception, every fragment which can be identified as a breech section is octagon. There are no known round breech sections. On the contrary, every known muzzle section is round. The round sections outnumber the octagon sections about three to one. Presumably, this is because many of the round sections come from the center sections of the gun barrel as well as from the muzzle. One muzzle section from 23Ve4 still has the front sight and is identical in size and design to the muzzle of my own Northwest Gun.

Most authorities dealing with the Indian trade seem to agree that, on the whole, the guns were of inferior quality; the barrels being particularly subject to criticism. On the other hand, both Russell and Hanson show that during the 19th Century, at least, the trading companies held their suppliers to rather rigid standards because the Indian was usually proficient in distinguishing between a good and a worthless gun. Hanson, particularly, quotes correspondence from factors to the home office, or the inspector, complaining bitterly about the last shipment and the number returned by the Indians for replacement.[6][7]

When these barrels were cut in two, it was found that only a good hacksaw would bite into them and then only with reluctance. It is difficult not to associate this toughness with outstanding tensile strength. Possibly an explanation for this is found in a quotation in Russell's notes taken from STONEHENGE in which he discusses the various grades of iron used in making gun barrels.

"Charcoal iron is the best quality used for inferior guns; it is made from the clippings of sheet-iron, melted in a charcoal furnace and then recast, then forged into a bar and rolled into rods in imitation of stub-twist. The iron when in contact with the charcoal absorbs a certain amount of carbon and becomes hardened, but as the metal from which it is made is originally of a weak description, it still remains of an inferior quality."[8]

Later, in the same notes, the comment is made that the method of making the barrel by twisting a flat strip of iron spirally around a mandril and forging the edges together was not developed until 1806.[9] Previous to that development, the only way to make a gun barrel was to start with a flat strip of iron, somewhat longer than the finished barrel, as wide as its circumference, and somewhat thicker than the final wall thickness. By bending the strip of iron along its longitudinal axis, first into a "U" shape, and finally into an "O", by inserting a mandril in the

Figure 37. Lead bullets and French gun flints from Little Osage site 23Sα3.

bore, the barrel itself was formed. The final operation was to forge the edges of the iron together into a welded seam, which was usually placed at the bottom of the barrel in the finished gun. The rough bore was cleaned up by rotating a "long bit" through it which produced a surprisingly smooth finish. Obviously, the bore diameters of individual barrels were not held to close tolerances, as we understand that term today.

A variation of the above, was to start with two strips, the width of each representing half the circumference of the barrel. These iron strips were first bent along their longitudinal axis into a semi-circular, or "C" shape, and then welded over a mandril. This resulted in two longitudinal welds running down the length of the barrel. It is interesting to note that there is one muzzle section from 23Vel which is one of these semicircular halves; the explosion which burst it apart followed the weld lines exactly. Whether a barrel with a double weld was supposed to be superior to one with only one longitudinal seam remains to be determined. However, unless the double seamed barrel was considered superior, it is difficult to understand why they went to the trouble and expense of doubling their work of welding.

The Northwest Gun became established as a type in the fur trade during the first decade of the 19th Century[10] and can be best described as a light musket. Its distinguishing feature, aside from its general outline, is a sideplate in the form of a highly stylized sea serpent. The breech of the barrel is always octagon, while the midsection and muzzle are round. There is not a definitely identifiable Northwest Gun barrel which measured more than one inch across the flats, and it is believed a safe assumption that any barrel breech greater than one inch is not from a 19th Century trade gun, but from either an 18th or 19th Century military musket or an 18th Century trade gun.

This assumption is strengthened by the fact that there are curved lockplates from these sites which were unquestionably made during the early 1700's (See Fig. 38, 1 and 4, p. 78). The probability is that the barrel breeches measuring 1 1/8 inches to 1 1/4 inches across the flats were originally associated with these early locks.

These gun barrels were broken up not because of a massacre, as Hill and other early students presumed, but to make fleshers and scrapers for removing flesh and fat from hides. Laubin in his book on the tipi describes the process in detail and illustrates the tools.[11] Barrel sections were also used as diggers and stakes.

Figure 38. Lockplates from Little Osage site 23Ve3.

The fourth plate from the top is an early 18th Century type and was probably made before 1750. Note the extreme curvature.

Since most of these barrel sections, if not flattened, have been deformed at the ends while being broken, it was necessary to cut some of them in half in an attempt to locate a more or less circular bore, as well as a spot where the attack of rust was at a minimum. It was hoped that the inner surfaces, guarded by a tight plug of dirt and removed from the ends, would be less rusted due to a more limited supply of oxygen. This assumption seems to have been a sound one.

Because of the difficulty encountered in sawing the barrel fragments, not all were cut. Where it seemed that a reliable measurement could be gotten from the broken end, the sawing was dispensed with.

The gauges and calibers shown in the tabulations on page 81 do not necessarily correspond to the hundredth of an inch with the caliper measurements given, but are those which seemed to be most logically assignable to the caliper readings. This approach was decided upon because any attempt to determine the exact original caliber of one of these barrels depended more upon one's judgement than upon the accuracy of his calipers. In some instances, the rust had built up the inner surfaces and in others it had eroded away. Therefore, all measurements were made with ordinary calipers measuring to 1/32nd of an inch.

The real weakness in using a gauge list to approximate the original bore is that no two lists agree. However, the important question is not whether a ball which weighed 24 to a pound measured .579 or .588 inches in diameter, but which gauge list was actually used by the manufacturers of the guns in question?

Frankly, that is a question to which a definite answer has not been found, but Steele and Harrison state that the list they show had been adopted by the English proofing companies. They do not say when the list was adopted and it is not presumed that it was in effect during the 1700's; however, it is the most authoritative gauge list found so far and is included here.

GAUGE LIST
ADOPTED BY THE LONDON PROOFING COMPANIES

Number of Gauge	Dia. of Bore,	Number of Gauge	Dia. of Bore,
1	1.669	19	.626
2	1.325	20	.615
3	1.157	21	.605

Number of Gauge	Dia. of Bore,	Number of Gauge	Dia. of Bore,
4	1.052	22	.596
5	.976	23	.587
6	.919	24	.579
7	.873	25	.571
8	.835	26	.563
9	.803	27	.556
10	.775	28	.550
11	.751	29	.543
12	.729	30	.537
13	.710	31	.531
14	.693	32	.526
15	.677	33	.520
16	.662	34	.515
17	.650	35	.510
18	.637	36	.506[12]

The system of specifying bore size by referring to the number of balls required to weigh a pound is both unwieldy and inexact. However, since it was in universal use with both smoothbores and rifles until well past the middle of the last century, we have no choice but to continue working within this same framework of reference when dealing with ancient gun barrels.

It is obvious that the diameter of a lead ball of a given weight will vary with the purity of the lead. Furthermore, working under the limits of inexact measurements and manufacturing techniques which necessarily prevailed into the 19th Century, the molds from which balls of a supposed diameter were made varied far from the theoretical norm. Consequently, it is not surprising to find that no two gauge lists agree.

To illustrate how this gauge list was used in actual practice, the closest decimal equivalent in hundredths of an inch to 19/32 is .59. Using this gauge list, .59 inch indicates 23 gauge. However, 24 and not 23 was a standard trade gun gauge. Since it is very unlikely that the caliper readings are accurate enough to justify the assumption that we are dealing with an hitherto unknown trade gun bore size, the gauge was changed to 24 and the probable caliber to .58.

In the following tabulation, the barrel fragments listed under "No measurement" were too badly deformed to be measured. Also, please note that there are a total of 33 barrel fragments in the Crick collection but ony five were available when the measurements were made.

DISTRIBUTION OF BORE SIZES FOUND
IN OSAGE INDIAN BARREL FRAGMENTS

Caliper Measure-ments	7/16	1/2	17/32	9/16	19/32	5/8	11/16	No Mea.
Probable Gauge	56	36	32	28	24	20	14	
Probable Caliber	.44	.50	.53	.55	.58	.62	.69	
From 23Ve4	0	1	0	2	1	0	0	0
From 23Ve3	0	3	4	4	0	1	1	6
From 23Ve1	5	30	10	30	5	9	0	82
From 23Sa3	0	2	0	1	1	1	0	?
Total 199	5	36	14	37	7	11	1	88

For site code identification refer to page 71.

The barrel fragment in the best condition is from 23Ve4. It is 28 gauge and 18 inches in length. The tang is broken off and the breech plug shows signs of having been battered. The barrel is bent slightly at the center. The octagon breech section, though rusted, still shows the flats distinctly; measuring 1 1/4 inches across the breech. The flats extend 8 1/2 inches up the barrel and apparently merged into the round portion without any decorative rings, as is charateristic of the Northwest Gun. The wall thickness at the muzzle calipers 5/32 inch. This barrel looks as if it came from a good, sturdy gun which was made to give honest service.

Since the breech section of those Northwest Gun barrels which have been examined never exceed one inch across the flats, it is possible that the breech dimensions of the barrel fragments may have some significance. The outer surfaces of these fragments are much more pocked and eroded by rust than the bores, probably because the inner surfaces were more protected from the oxygen in the soil. Consequently, in many instances the flats must be located by a sort of general overall impression, rather than by actually seeing them. It follows, then, that these measurements across the breech flats are all less than the original dimensions and many are well below.

MINIMUM DISTANCES ACROSS THE FLATS OF REPRESENTATIVE BREECH SECTIONS FROM OSAGE VILLAGE SITES. MEASUREMENTS BY CALIPER TO 1/32nd OF AN INCH.

Gauge	56	36	32	28	24	20	14
Bore	.44	.50	.53	.55	.58	.62	.69
From 23Ve4	0	0	0	1-1/4	0	1-3/16	0
From 23Ve3	0	0	0	0	0	1-3/16	1-7/32
From 23Vel	0	15/16	1-1/32	1	1-1/32	0	0
		1-1/32		1-1/16	1-5/32		
		1-1/8		1-1/4	1-1/16		
					1		
					1-1/8		
					1-3/16		

The .44 caliber bore is the only size which does not have a single breech section that can be identified with it. There is one badly eroded breech section which may have been .44 caliber originally but could also have been .50. It now measures one inch across the flats. Strangely, some of the surfaces of the flats on this particular fragment are still in fair condition and it is doubtful whether the original dimension exceeded 1-1/16 inches.

BULLETS

Of the sixteen bullets in the Crick collection, fourteen have not been shot and reasonably accurate measurements were taken from them. The other three are deformed, but their caliber can be approximated by weighing. Actually, these bullets are in surprisingly good condition and oxidation of the surface is not a problem. As is usual with moulds of that period, most of the bullets cast are ovoid, rather than round, and it is pointless to use anything more accurate than calipers measuring to 1/32 of an inch in trying to determine the diameter.

The weight variations within the same gauge are probably due to differences in the purity of the lead as well as irregularities in the moulds used in casting them.

The last bullet listed is either a buckshot or a rifle ball. It is also cast, ovoid in shape and measures with the micrometer .310 inch by .325

inch. Since no rifle barrels have been found on any of the Osage sites, it is most probably a buckshot. Furthermore, it is of a very light caliber for a frontier rifle, since the light calibered rifles did not make their appearance until after the frontier, with its larger game animals, had passed a given area.

Caliper Measurement	Probable Gauge	Weight in Grams
17/32"	32	13.4
		15.4
		16.5
		15.3
		15.5 (from 23Ve3)
9/16"	28	15.0
		15.5
		15.5
		17.0
		17.3
		17.2
		17.55
		17.9
		17.6 (from 23Ve3)
		17.5 (from 23Ve3)
19/32"	24	19.9
		19.0
5/16"	50	3.5

SUMMARY ON BULLETS AND BARRELS

Referring back to the tabulation on gun barrels, the smaller calibers are very puzzling, since no known trade guns of such light gauges have been reported. Hanson says that the calibers on forty trade guns made during the 19th Century and examined by him ranged from .58 to .62[13] A careful examination of Russell also fails to reveal any references to guns of .50 inch or .52 inch bores.[14] Furthermore, since these guns were used as often with shot as with ball, gauges of 32 or 36—not to mention 56—seem entirely too small to be practical.

However, confident that the measurements are reasonably accurate, it is safe to assume that the original bores were actually as small as indicated. Additional research and study may eventually identify them, but for the moment the only explanation which occurs is that possibly they are the elusive relics of the unknown French trade guns of the late 17th and early 18th Centuries.

The same conclusions may apply to the barrels of .55 caliber or 28 gauge, but that bore is beginning to approach a size more nearly compatible with the recognized sizes of 24 and 20 gauge.

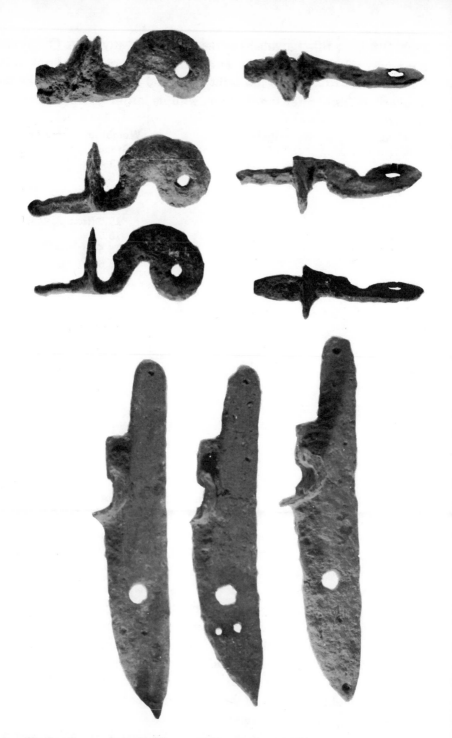

Figure 39. Locks and cocks from Little Osage 23Ve4.
By carefully cleaning and polishing the tail of the bottom lock, the letters "NE" of the name "BARNETT" could be made out.

Since bullets are often found, but no barrels, it is important to determine which size ball fits which bore. Does it necesssarily follow, for instance, that a 24 gauge ball was used in a 24 gauge barrel?

There is not much known about the loading practices with smoothbores except that James Willard Schultz, in a letter to Charles E. Hanson, Jr., stated that they patched the ball, using a 30 gauge ball in a 24 gauge bore. Schultz did not say what patch material was used, but Hanson advances a personal hypothesis that it was striped ticking, since the records show that it was a staple item of trade during the mid-1800's.[15]

Of course, Schultz was thinking of the Northwest Trade Guns and a period possibly 100 years later than the older barrels concerned with here. When the older guns were in use it is much more probable that well worn doeskin was the prevailing patching material. However, there may not have been too great a difference in thickness between the two materials.

The theoretical difference in diameters between 24 and 30 gauge is .04 inches. Recognizing for the moment that the actual ball diameters, would vary a hundredth or so one way or the other because of the manufacturing methods of the 18th Century, the fact still remains that a diameter difference between the ball and the bore of .03 and .04 inch would give a rather loose fit with ticking or something similar as the patching material.

Based on rifle shooting experience, it is known that a diameter difference between ball and bore of .005 inch is ample when using ticking .021 inch thick. Actually, a clearance of from .003 down to zero is preferable; but that is dealing with extremely accurate round ball target rifles in which the bores are cleaned between each shot. A smoothbore would undoubtedly require more clearance, probably about .02 inch. The following tabulation seems to support this hypothesis.

Comparison of balls found on Little Osage site 23SA3 with bores they were most probably intended to fit:

Probable Gauge of Balls	32	28	24
Balls Theoretical Diameter	.526"	.550"	.579"

Average Diameters	.53"(17/32)	.56"(9/16)	.59"(19/32)
Gauge of Guns	28	24	20
Guns Theoretical Bore Diameter	.550"	.579"	.615"
Difference	.024	.029	.036

LOCKS AND LOCKPLATES

The lockplates from the Vernon County sites are all stripped down to the pan. Nothing else is left on them. Just what this signifies is open to argument, but there must be some reason behind this peculiarity. This systematic stripping of parts seems to indicate that the Indians were using the parts for repair of other locks still in active service. This is strengthened by the fact that some gunsmithing tools have also been found, such as the handvise from Big Osage site 23Ve1. Files, both three cornered and flat, have also been found and it is possible that some of the unidentified metal items are either screwdrivers or gouges.

The locks and lockplates from Little Osage site 23Sa3, in contrast, all have their frizzen springs as well as their pans. One lock is complete except for its frizzen. There is one lockplate which still has its frizzen, frizzen spring and mainspring.

Lockplate No. 7 from Big Osage site 23Ve1 is the only instance in either the collections or the Gunsmith's Cache where a bridled frizzen was found. The bridle is badly rusted, but it is still attached to the pan and plainly visible. Since the tentative termination date of this site is 1815, this bridled frizzen fits perfectly into the dating pattern.

At one time it was thought that perhaps some of the frizzen pivot screws were supported by a link anchoring on the frizzen spring screw, as on the model 1717 French military locks, but no notched frizzen springs were found.

SIDEPLATES

Sideplates are one of the most promising of all gun parts for diagnostic use.

Figure 40. Lockplates from Big Osage site 23Ve1.

These lockplates from 23Ve1, with an indicated occupational period of 1790-1815 from documentary evidence, are deeply pocked with rust. The bottom plate was the only one which looked as if it would respond to treatment. After carefully removing the rust and treating with acid, enough was legible to show that it was a Barnett lock made in 1805. Lockplates No. 2 and No. 5 were held to the stock with three sidescrews. All others were two sidescrew plates.

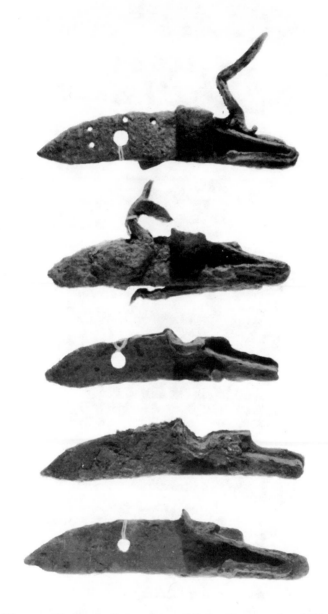

Figure 41. Lockplates from Little Osage site 23Sa3.

To clean either a flintlock or a caplock gun the first step is to remove the lock. The flintlock is held to the gun with either two or three sidescrews which pass entirely through the stock, while the caplock is usually mounted with only one sidescrew. In both instances, the head of each screw is prevented from sinking into the wood by a plate of some description mounted on the side opposite the lockplate. This is the sideplate and it may be ornamental in the extreme, or may be only a simple washer. Though there are exceptions, in the flintlock era a simple sideplate is usually found on military weapons; sporting and trade guns having more ornamental ones.

Just how the distinctive serpent or dragon sideplate evolved during the 18th Century, to become the trademark of the 19th Century Northwest Gun, is still subject to debate. Russell discusses this problem thoroughly.[16] The final form is well illustrated by the three fragments forming the third line of objects in Figure 42. Though they may not all be from the same sideplate originally, each piece is of approximately the correct length to fit together properly.

The three fragments forming the top line of objects in the same illustration probably represent steps in this evolutionary line, and approximate the original design. They are not cast, as the later serpent sideplates were, but are made of flat brass with the design engraved on the surface. They should bear a tentative date of about 1750.

The cast brass serpent sideplates probably date from 1780 to 1790 at the very earliest. On the whole, they are charateristic of the 19th Century trade gun in its final form and, only under exceptional circumstances can they be assumed to antedate 1800.

In the collections, there are two plain iron sideplates, four sideplates of engraved sheet brass about 1/16 inch thick, and ten serpent sideplates of cast brass. By "sideplates" either complete plates or fragments are indicated. Tabulation by sites is as follows:

SIDEPLATE DISTRIBUTION BY SITES AND PRESUMED OCCUPATIONS

Site	Presumed Occupation	Iron Sideplates	Engraved Serpent Sideplates	Cast Serpent Sideplates
23Sa3	1730-1775	2	1	1
23Ve4	1775-1815	0	0	0
23Ve3	—1775—	0	0	1
23Ve1	1790-1815	0	3	8

Figure 42. Broken sections of serpent sideplates arranged in their original order.

The three lower pieces are interesting examples of early sideplates made from flat brass with the design engraved into the surface. The two upper rows are from cast sideplates and are representative of the final form. From Big Osage site 23Ve1.

BUTTPLATES AND MISCELLANEOUS GUN FURNITURE

The probabilities are that a flat brass buttplate came from a North-west Gun, though they were not the first to use them. Hanson states that the first Northwest buttplates were held to the stock with nails.[17] In about 1826 the Hudson Bay fukes (trade gun) began using five screws—four in the plate and one in the tang—while trade guns sold in the United States, even though of British manufacture, had only two screws; one in the plate and one in the tang. Therefore, this particular form of buttplate offers rather reliable dating information, but is not too indicative of origin, except in the case of a five screw plate. Figure 43, page 92, illustrates three types of buttplate found on Big Osage site 23Ve1; A and B being seven nail, C a six nail, and D is the bottom end of a two screw plate.

Item C in Figure 44 is a complete iron buttplate with the tang bent over against the inner, or convex side. It, as well as the other three buttplate fragments shown, are of iron and badly rust covered. They were all held to the stock with two screws; one where shown on butt-plate C, the other screw hole being in the corner of the right angled bend between the tang and the plate proper. One half of the screw hole in A shows plainly in the photograph since the break between tang and plate passed directly through it. These iron buttplates are all from Little Osage site 23Sa3.

The only other site with an iron buttplate is Big Osage 23Ve3. Here is an upper buttplate finial Figure 44, D, very similar in general outline to A, mentioned in the preceding paragraph, and equally rusted.

23Sa3 is also well represented with fragments of brass buttplates. The last two items on the first and second rows (Fig. 45) are all butt-plate finials. The third item, first row, is particularly noteworthy since its design is a bow and quiver. Furthermore, it is distinctly an Indian bow in outline, impressionistically drawn, it is true, but definitely not an English longbow.

The center item in the second row has the letter "A" above a stand of four flags about a vertical lance with a pennant. Unfortunately, the break occurs at the point where the flags and lance cross, so the bottom of the sketch is lost. It is very similar though in general treatment to the stand of flags and drums shown by George[18]. This indicates possibly English origin, but there is a French "feel" in the design outline.

Figure 43. Buttplates from Big Osage site 23Ve1.

In the upper row, the first two are an early type Northwest Gun buttplate requiring seven square nails to hold them to the stock. The third plate used six nails. Only the tip of the fourth buttplate is present and was probably held by one screw in the plate and one in the tang. Since the edges are rounded more than is customarily found on Northwest Guns, this plate may have come from an earlier firearm. The lower row illustrates two views of cast buttplates. There is a possibility that the plate to the left was from a rifle. The other was from a heavy military type musket.

Figure 44. Buttplates and Gun Decorations, Little Osage site, 23Ve3.

Upper row: Two iron finials and one complete iron buttplate from 23Sa3.

Lower row: An iron buttplate finial. The item next to it is a section of a brass trigger guard.

The upper object to the extreme right is the head of a serpent sideplate. Below it the finial of a brass trigger guard, while the bottom object is part of a file.

Fig. 45. Fragments of brass gun furniture from Osage sites.

TOP ROW: 1 & 2, trigger guard finials from 2Sa3. Items 3 & 4, buttplate finials from 23Sa3. Item 3 has a quiver crossed with a bow.

SECOND ROW: Item 1 is the wide bow of a trigger guard which has been flattened and drilled at one end for suspension. Item 2 is the finial of a buttplate with the letter "A" engraved in the center. Below the "A" are two flags crossed with a lance. Unfortunately, the piece is broken at the point where the flags cross. Item 3 is another buttplate finial with a thistle—a popular English design. All items on second row from 23Sa3.

THIRD ROW: The first item is a buttplate finial with an abstract design, similar to a wreath. The second item is another buttplate finial with a design resembling the bud of a tulip. This has been tentatively identified as Spanish. All items on this row from Big Osage 23Vel.

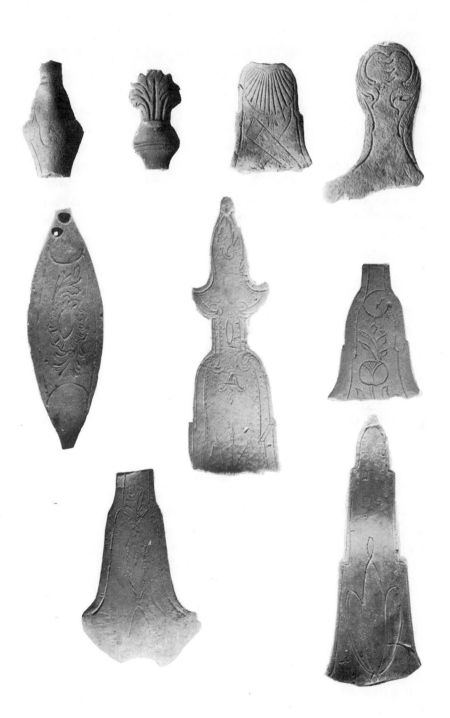

There are two brass buttplate finials from 23Ve3; one of which is particularly noteworthy. The last item, bottom row, Fig. 45, appears to one of our outstanding authorities, Stephen V. Grancsay of the Metropolitan Museum of Art, New York City, to be "Spanish in form". This does not mean necessarily that it is of Spanish origin, but is an interesting possibility since it is the first indication that Spanish firearms might be represented on these Osage village sites.[19]

Figure 43, items E and F, illustrate two buttplates from 23Ve1 of unusual form. E is ruggedly made of cast brass and inner surfaces plainly showing the rough face from the sand mold. The upper corner, where the plate proper and the tang join, is sharp and recurved, while the plate has the curve of a rifle plate. The overall length of the buttplate is very close to that which it had been originally, but there has been some hacking or cutting at the lower end. Though it seems a trifle wide, it could be classified as a rifle buttplate. If it actually is from a rifle, here is the first evidence found that the Osage had that type of firearm.

Item F is a big cast brass buttplate which has been hammered and battered out of shape. The finial is gone. It was probably held to the stock with a tongue and pin, while the plate proper was held by a single screw. It is from a large smoothbore.

TRIGGER GUARDS

There are six remnants of iron trigger guards from Little Osage site 23Sa3.

Figure 46, A, from 23Sa3, is the bow section of a brass trigger guard, remarkably free from decoration.

Item B from Big Osage site 23Ve1, is another brass trigger guard, identical in outline to A. Though both are severely plain in decoration, they are not the same and are not from the same pattern. However, it is interesting to find two items, so similar, coming from different sites with corresponding occupation dates.

CONCLUSION

This brief study of gun parts found on four Osage village sites shows that the respective indicated dates of manufacture correspond reasonably well with the presumed occupational periods. The best correlation is with the parts from Northwest Guns; probably because that is the one gun type with which we are well acquainted at this time. There is every reason to believe, as 18th Century trade gun types become recognized and established, that these older gun parts will become valuable aids in determining the limits of historic occupational periods.

The locks and lockplates which were expected to yield the most information in the determination of origin, remain the most enigmatic. On the other hand, the gun barrel fragments, which originally appeared to be the least promising, have had great diagnostic possibilities.

A reasonably accurate determination of the original bore size can be made so long as there is an inch or two of the barrel fragment which has not been deformed by flattening or breaking. This is particularly true if the bore is well plugged with dirt to exclude oxygen and reduce the rusting process on bore surfaces. The outside measurements are more questionable due to the greater erosion from rust, but judgment combined with experience can produce relatively reliable dimensions for comparative purposes.

The greatest surprise has been the large percentage of bore diameters below .58 caliber, or 24 gauge; the smaller of the two standard bores used during the first half of the 19th Century. Out of a total of 111 barrel fragments measured, we find .50 caliber (36 gauge) and .55 caliber (28 gauge) each representing 30 percent of the total. Only 6.3 percent are .58 caliber (24 gauge) and 10 percent are .62 caliber (20 gauge). Most amazing of all—5 (or 4.6 percent of the total number measured) are .44 caliber (56 gauge).

Since smoothbores of such small gauges are completely unknown in the literature dealing with trade guns of the 19th Century, and there is practically nothing known about the trade guns of the 18th Century, the only reasonable conclusion seems to be that these are most probably from guns made before 1775.

Therefore, Big Osage site 23Vel may have been occupied long before 1790, since it has so many small bore barrel fragments. Its initial date can be estimated at least as early as 1750, and suggests that these smaller bored trade guns were of French origin.

1. Chapman, Carl H. (1946) THE MISSOURI ARCHAEOLOGIST, Vol. 10, p.16.
2. Chappell, Phil E. (1902) "Malta Bend Qui Vive", MISSOURI VILLAGE.
3. Hill, Ed C. (1914) "Has The Site of Fort Orleans Been Discovered?", MISSOURI HISTORICAL COLLECTIONS, Vol. IV, pp. 367-369.

4. Berry, B., Chapman, C.H., and Mack, J. (1944) "The Archaeological Remains of the Osage", AMERICAN ANTIQUITY, vol. 10, pp. 1-11.
5. Chapman, C.H., Personal Letter.
6. Russell, Carl P. (1957) GUNS ON THE EARLY FRONTIER.
7. Hanson, Chas. E., Jr. (1955) THE NORTHWEST GUN.
8. Russell, op. cit., p. 314, (STONEHENGE, 1859, p. 218).
9. ibid.
10. Hanson, op. cit.
11. Laubin, Reginald (1957) THE INDIAN TIPI, pp. 68-73
12. Steele, J.P. and Harrison, Wm. B. (1883) THE GUNSMITH'S MANUAL, New York, p. 135
13. Hanson, Chas. E., Jr. (1957) Personal Letter, Feb. 11.
14. Russell, op. cit.
15. Hanson, Chas. E., Jr. (1958) Personal Letter, Mar. 18 (Schultz, Jas. Willard, Letter to Hanson).
16. Russell, op. cit., pp. 127-130.
17. Hanson, op. cit., p. 40.
18. George, J.N. (1947) ENGLISH GUNS AND RIFLES.
19. Grancsay, Stephen V. (1958) Personal Letter, Nov. 18.
20. Peterson, Harold L. (1956) ARMS AND ARMOR IN COLONIAL AMERICA, 1526-1783, pp. 161 and 167.

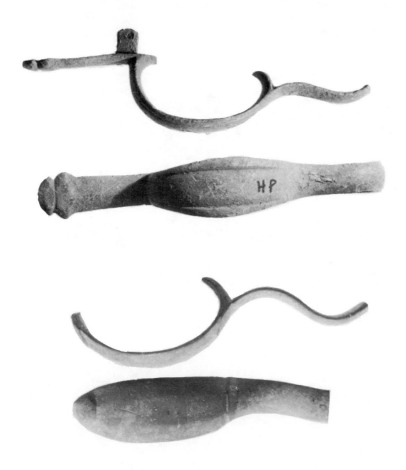

Figure 46. Two brass trigger guards.
The upper, from Little Osage 23Sa3 and the lower from Big Osage 23Ve1.
The assigned occupational dates, based upon documentary evidence, are 1730-1775
and 1790-1815, respectively.

Figure 47. Gun flints from Little Osage site 23Sa3.

These are all of native manufacture with the exception of two. The first flint in the second row is an English pistol or rifle flint, and in the third row, the fourth flint is a gun spall.

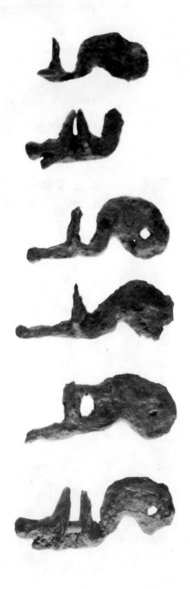

Figure 48. Cocks from Big Osage site 23Ve1.

Figure 49. Cocks, frizzens, trigger plates and upper vise jaw from Big Osage site 23Ve3.

A front view of the cocks is shown in lower right hand corner.

102

Figure 50. Gunsmithing tools from Big Osage site 23Ve1, tentative occupational date, 1790-1815.

The first three items are sections from three-cornered and flat files. The diagonally placed object is, in all probability, the blade of a chisel used to inlet lock into stock. Object on bottom is a hand vise.

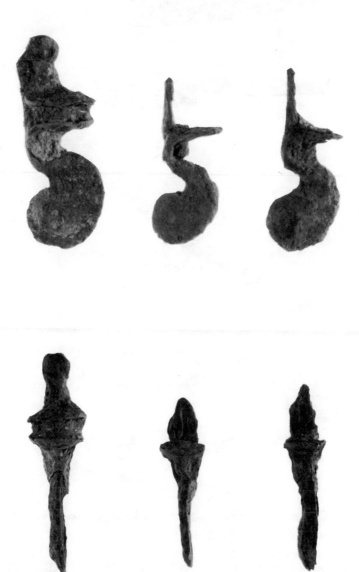

104

Figure 51. Front and side views of cocks from Little Osage site 23Sa3.

The left cock is probably from a second model English Tower, or Brown Bess musket of the 1760-1778 period. this is one of the few cocks from Indian sites which can be identified with reasonable accuracy. This cock measured approximately three inches from center of tumbler screw to top of comb. (See illustration in Peterson, 1956. Peterson describes the evolution of the Brown Bess cock as follows: *"In the first model and early years of second model [introduced about 1760], a tenon on the top jaw of the flint vise slid in a mortise in the tang of the cock. In later years on the second model, a slot was cut in the back of the jaw so that it fitted around the tang, which had been modified somewhat to make this possible. Finally, whereas the head of the flint screw on the first two models was slotted only, the head of the screw of the third model [introduced about 1778] was both slotted and pierced."*[20] This particular cock not only has the shape and size of the second model Brown Bess cock, but the flint vise upper jaw is fitted around the comb, or "tang" as Peterson calls it. Since the flint screw is not pierced, but only slotted, it is a late second model cock and was probably made around 1770. The other two cocks are from light smoothbores, in all probability. Both have mortised combs, which, combined with the extreme erosion from rust, indicates a date of 1750 or earlier.

Chapter 7
Indian Trade Gun Locks from the 19th Century
by
Charles E. Hanson, Jr.

The extensive collection of Indian trade guns in the Museum of the Fur Trade (Chadron, Nebraska) includes several interesting specimens. Parts of trade guns are found rather infrequently in the Rocky Mountain regions where the Indians had no fixed village sites. When the remains of guns are found, they very often occur with the skeletons of the last owners, either in burials or on the sites of fatal encounters with men or beasts.

Considered in chronological order, the specimens in the Museum furnish a thumbnail story of the "Northwest Gun" in 19th Century America.

The lockplate by Ketland of Birmingham (Fig. 52, p. 108) is the only middle-western find in the group. It was discovered years ago in northern Ohio and has apparently been through a fire. The interior parts of the lock remain, but the hammer, frizzen spring, frizzen and replaceable powder pan are all gone. Exact details of the situation in which the lock was found are lacking. It has passed through several hands since that time.

Ketland was a noted maker of Northwest Guns for the old Northwest Company of Montreal . The firm of Ketland & Company was established at Birmingham in the 1740's by William Ketland and was continued by his descendants until 1831. Like some other early Birmingham makers, this firm established a private proof house and its mark, crossed scepters under a crown, was the pattern for the official Birmingham Proof House mark adopted in 1813. This was another tribute to the high reputation held by Ketland & Company. The Ketlands manufactured tools, parts, locks, and whole guns of superior quality. Their locks, pistols and smooth bore muskets were very highly regarded in America.[1]

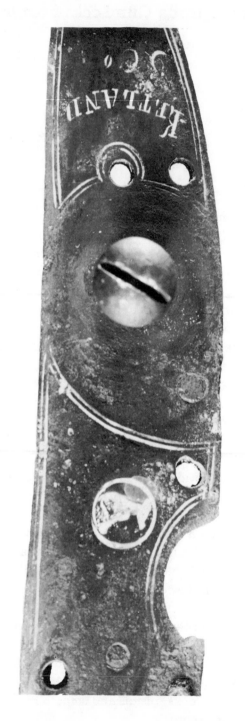

Figure 52. Lockplate by Ketland of Birmingham, England, found in Ohio.

Note "fox-in-circle" viewing mark believed to have been the special mark of the Northwest Company.

In 1809, the Superintendent of the U.S. Office of Indian Trade was ordering "real North West guns by Barnett or Ketland." In 1808, the same office had imported 25 dozen Ketland locks for the use of American riflesmiths making firearms for sale to the Indians.

There is no record of Ketland muskets being sold by the Hudson's Bay Company.

The subject lockplate is 6 1/8 inches long, stamped "Ketland & Co." on the tail and marked with an early type of "fox in circle" viewer's mark. This circle mark is believed to have been the special mark of the Northwest Company.

The ancient Northwest Gun (Fig. 53, A and B) is a rare Hudson's Bay Company musket dated 1820—a year before the Hudson's Bay Company amalgamation with the Northwest Company. This gun was found in 1911 by a sheepherder in the ruins of a stone Indian fort high in the Owl Creek Mountains of Wyoming. It reposed for many years thereafter in the lobby of the Teton Hotel in Riverton, Wyoming.

The wood stock is naturally much deteriorated but the metal parts have remained surprisingly clean in the dry mountain air. "Wilson, 1820" shows clearly on the tail of the lockplate and the "tombstone fox" viewer's mark of the Hudson's Bay Company—is faintly discernible under the pan.

The part-octagon barrel is 31 inches long and has been cut down considerably. The unbridled lock is 6 1/8 inches long and has a gooseneck cock and replaceable pan held on by screws. There are three side screws and the tang screw comes upward from the front of the guard to engage the barrel tang. The lock is typical of trade guns in the 1770-1821 period; after 1821 forged pans, tumbler and frizzen trigger plate gradually became common.

In general, the other features of this fusil—trigger guard, barrel, and brass serpent sideplate—are typical of all Northwest Guns.

Wilson began making guns for the Hudson's Bay Company in 1731 and continued with few interruptions until 1833. From 1821-24 and 1826-33 Wilson, the former prime supplier to the Hudson's Bay Company, and Barnett, former prime supplier to the Northwest Company, were both making guns for the newly reorganized Hudson's Bay Company.[2]

This particular specimen might well have been the weapon of some Blackfoot warrior who came to central Wyoming with a war party

Figure 53. Left and Right views of three 19th Century Trade Guns.
A & B: An 1820 English trade gun made for the Hudson's Bay Company by Wilson of London. Found in a stone "fort" in the Owl Creek Mountains of Wyoming. The fort was probably made by a Blackfoot war party.
C & D: A Belgian trade gun found in the Heart Mountains, Wyoming, stamped "Barnet, 1848" on tail of lock. Imitation Hudson's Bay Company viewer's mark in front of cock.
E & F: Remains of an 1838 Belgian trade gun found in a sand dune on the Red Desert of Southwestern Wyoming. Stamped "Barnett, 1838" on tail of lock. In front of cock is an imitation Northwest Company mark—a sitting fox in a circle.

against the Snakes or against a band of Mountain Men. Blackfoot war parties very often built the kind of stone "fort" in which the gun was found.[3] Since most fusils lasted only a few years in Indian hands, we might surmise that the supposed war expedition occurred about 1825.

The third specimen (Fig. 53, E and F) was found in a sand dune on the Red Desert north of Rock Springs, Wyoming, in 1956. The wooden stock was completely disintegrated and all that remained were the barrel, lock, sideplate and trigger. The mainspring in the lock is broken and the gun may possibly have been thrown away in haste when the break occurred.

It is typical of the better-quality Belgian guns imported by the American Fur Company in the 1830's. The 6 1/4 inch lock is stamped "Burnett, 1838" on the tail and has a "fox in circle" with the letters "IA". These marks are particularly interesting. The "Burnett" is intended to imitate the English "Barnett" as closely as possible. The viewmark combines the old Northwest Company "fox in circle" with the letters "IA" ordinarily used in the tombstone fox mark on Northwest Guns made for sale in the United States.

The barrel imitates a Barnett barrel, with two "Birmingham" proofmarks and "TB" with a star, on the left flat (Thomas Barnett usually placed his initials with a star on his Northwest Company fusils). The top barrel flat carries the word "London" and the same "fox in circle" with "IA" that appears on the lock.

The lock itself is of good quality and typical of those used in the 1830-45 period, with bridled pan and tumbler, two lock screws or "bolts" and sturdy rounded gooseneck hammer.

The 42 inch barrel is original length with original front sight and three "wire loops". These loops will be be noted in the photograph. They are the small lugs brazed on the barrel to receive small pins or "wires" driven through the stock. On better quality guns, the lugs have a rectangular opening to receive flat keys and were known as "bolt lugs".

Like most 19th Century Northwest Guns, this one is about .59 caliber or 24 gauge. Balls in 30 gauge or .53 caliber were sold at most trading posts for use with patch or wadding in the smooth bore fusils.

Nothing was found with this gun to indicate its exact origin but it was probably sold at Fort Laramie to a Sioux warrior. Another possibility might be that it was a Shoshone gun purchased at a traders' rendezvous.

The last of our series is also a Belgian gun (Fig. 53, C and D). The fact is not surprising, for next to the products of W. Chance (Birmingham), Belgian guns were the most common firearms, sold by the Chouteaus. The Fort Union inventories for 1850 list, "27 Belgian guns, 13 Belgian guns used, and 2 N.W. guns used."

This weathered veteran was found some sixty years ago by the late Ned Frost, famous Wyoming guide and hunter, and passed directly from Mr. Frost to the Museum. He found it leaning against the wall of a cave high on the side of Heart Mountain, Wyoming. Nearby was the sitting skeleton of a man which was not recovered, for Frost never returned to the spot again.

The gun is a very good Belgian imitation of the famous English Barnett Northwest Gun. The six inch lock is stamped "Barnett, 1848" on the tail and has the "tombstone fox" on lock and barrel. Under the fox are the letters "IR" used by some foreign makers on guns made for the American Fur Company and its successors.[4]

The 36 1/2 inch barrel is apparently original length for it has three "wire loops" and original front sight. It has two fake London proofmarks (very crude with no details on the crowns) and "London" on the top flat. Underneath it carried the familiar Belgian proofmark, "ELG" in an oval. The general details of sideplate, barrel and lock are typical of the 1830-55 period: gooseneck hammer on bridled lock, with barrel octagon changing to sixteen-sided ending in two turned rings, then round for about three inches, then a fancy series of turned rings, then round tapering to muzzle. The weathered stock has the marks of several lines of brass tacks and one square tack shank is still embedded.

This fusil is typical of those being sold on the far Western frontier by P. Chouteau Jr. & Company in the heyday of the Indian trade. It might have belonged to a Crow, a Blackfoot, a Gros Ventre or a Shoshone and was probably sold at Fort Union or some other post on the Missouri. Such guns were sold all through the 1850's until they were finally crowded off the market by cheap sturdy percussion rifles from Lancaster. By that time most of the Plains Indians were aligned on one side or the other in the last desperate struggle for supremacy with the white men crowding in from every side, and the Northwest Gun was laid aside for weapons with more power and accuracy.

[1] See BRITISH PISTOLS AND GUNS, 1640-1840, Ian Glendenning, 1951, Caswell & Co. Ltd. London. p. 180.

[2] See the NORTHWEST GUN, Charles E. Hanson, Jr., Nebraska State Historical Society, Lincoln, Nebraska, 1955, p. 18.

[3] Such forts of logs or stones were customary with most Rocky Mountain tribes. The writer has examined several of them in Northern Wyoming. See Fremont's note in THE DARING ADVENTURES OF KIT CARSON AND FREMONT, 1885, Hurst & Co., N.Y., p. 205; also Rufus B. Sage, ROCKY MOUNTAIN LIFE, 1857, Donohue, Hennebery & Co., Chicago, pp. 146-157

[4] There is a theory that the "IA" stands for Jacob Astor. See Hanson op. cit. p. 38.

Chapter 8
Relics From Fort Pierre II, Oahe Reservoir, South Dakota
by
Warren W. Caldwell

The data and analyses presented here focus upon a largely neglected aspect of aboriginal and frontier life. In contemporary accounts firearms and their necessary accouterments are considered as the common articles of daily use, and as such, worthy of no special comment. There is slight suggestion of detail, type, mode, or effectiveness in service. Even in the invoices of traders and inventories of government agencies, little can be found beyond statements of quantity and cost. The problem is of particular importance since firearms document so well the expansion of the frontier and concomitant shrinking and alteration of the aboriginal way of life. Dr. Carl Russell has presented an abundance of useful firearms data, but in terms of what can be added to the record, only the merest beginning has been made. While some have not been unaware of the problem, firearms, of necessity, have often been treated in a cursory manner. The Plains area has been something of an exception. Here there is a particularized, recent and observable continuity between the ethnographic present and the historic past. Firearms and associated paraphernalia have bulked so large in the fur trade and in recurrent warfare that the identification of specimens is of unusual importance.[1]

The artifacts described were recovered during the excavation of Ft. Pierre II, located on the west bank of the Missouri River just below the Oahe damsite in Stanley County, South Dakota. The excavations were carried out during the summer of 1956 by a Missouri Basin Project, Smithsonian Institution, field party under the direction of G. Hubert Smith. The excavations and analyses were part of the continuing effort to salvage cultural remains which were to be destroyed by water control projects in the Missouri River Basin.[2]

Ft. Pierre II was constructed as a post of the American Fur Company

("P. Chouteau, Jr., and Company") and occupied during the short interval of 1859-1863. Subsequently, U.S. army troops, detached from Ft. Sully I, may have been stationed in the area, 1863-1865. It is possible that they were encamped at the time on or near the area excavated in 1956.

I Firearms (See Fig. 54) (Numbers are catalog numbers in Missouri Basin Project Collections.)
A—Lock parts—
39ST217-900: Lockplate, badly rusted, no markings discernible, plate narrow and quite thin, rounded rear margin, outer surface smoothly beveled toward edges.
Two side screws, pan forged integral with plate, flash or drip fence at rear, reenforced bridle, frizzen spring intact, no roller-bearing at feather end.
Length—5.96", Width—1.15", Thickness—0.18"
Diameter of tumbler axle hole: ca. 0.4 inch.
Remarks—probably from a Northwest Gun.

39ST217-378: Fragment of a mainspring, tumbler-bearing surface missing, badly rusted.
Length—1.95", Width—0.46", Mean thickness of arm—0.19"
Remarks—too large to equate to the lockplate above, probably from large musket.

B—Trigger guard—
39ST217-1252: Trigger guard badly bent, iron, but metal reduced to oxide, elongated teardrop finials, deep bow, countersunk screw holes (just in front of bow, also 0.75 inch behind bow), rear tang straight (4.4 inches), short forward extension (2.5 inches).
Remarks—depth of bow, position of tang screw and material of manufacture indicate a Northwest Gun.

C—Buttplates—
39ST217-1040: Fragmentary, brass, with rounded toe and parallel sides, roughly finished, unbeveled edges, four roughly drilled and irregularly countersunk screw holes (two ca. 1.0 inches above toe, two presumably just below heel of stock).
Width—1.72", Thickness—0.09"
Remarks—shape, finish, and pattern of attachment indicate a buttplate from a Northwest Gun.

39ST217-1039: Two buttplate fragments, brass, roughly finished unbeveled edges, roughly bored and irregularly countersunk screw hole just above toe.
Width—1.55", Thickness—0.06"
Remarks—from a Northwest Gun.

D—Ramrod guides or pipes—
39ST217-1043: Tubular, copper, irregular annular ribbing on lower portion of body, bent from sheet copper, point of juncture continued as a narrow laminated flange (pierced by small central hole for attachment), flange stamped *CC*.
Length—1.24", Diameter—0.5"
Remarks—ramrod guide from a Northwest Gun.

39ST217-212: Same as above, but crushed, flange stamp obscured but probably *CC*.
Length—1.19"
Remarks—from a Northwest Gun.

The materials described above indicate the presence of at least two Northwest Guns, one of which is assuredly English in origin. Such firearms, produced by English, and later by American and Belgian workshops, were a staple in the western fur trade throughout the major span of its existence. As a mature, functional type, the gun was well established by the late 18th Century, persisting with only minor constructional alterations until the substantial stabilization of the American West in the late 1800's.[3] Minor changes or improvements in pattern provide some basis for placement of specific specimens in time.

Until 1860 the lockplate (flintlock) was slightly rounded on the external surface, but with a pointed tail at the rear. Subsequent specimens have a rounded rear termination.[4] The Ft. Pierre II specimen falls into the latter category. Pans are also variable. No reenforcing bridle, such as is present on the example above, occurs until after the 1820 period.[5] Similarly, until that date three lock screws were usual. Later, the rear screw does not appear.[6]

Northwest Guns characteristically had flat buttplates of brass with a short heel tang folded onto the top of the buttstock.[7] Only the lower or toe portions are present in the Ft. Pierre II collection. Buttplates were

Figure 54. Northwest Gun and parts and gun flints.
A—A typical Northwest Gun. B & D—Iron trigger guard from Northwest Gun.
C—Lockplate from Northwest Gun. E & F—Brass buttplates from Northwest Guns.
G—Fragment of lockspring from Northwest Gun. H—Ramrod guide from Northwest
Gun. I—Musket flint, French type. J—Rifle flint, English type. K—Pistol flint, English
type.

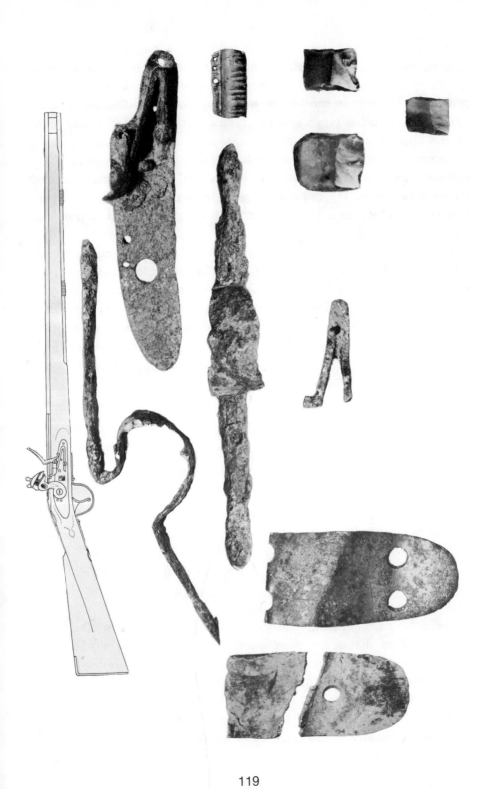

fixed to the stock with nails as late as 1826. Later specimens, particularly those distributed by the Hudson's Bay Company, utilized five screws, four around the butt and one in the heel tang.[8] At least one of the Ft. Pierre II specimens appears to be of this sort. The other example assuredly falls in the two-screw group (one in butt, one in tang) "Found on all other types sold or given out in the United States, even on the English-made models."[9]

Ramrod pipes do not appear to be reliable temporal criteria.[10] The ribbed copper rod tubes seem to be universal and characteristic over a long time range. Trigger guards seem to be more sensitive for by the late 18th Century guard finials had been lengthened and so persisted until the end of manufacture.

In total, the dateable specimens from Ft. Pierre II seem to be late ones, but entirely commensurate with the known occupation of the post. The distinctive fragments indicate at least one late trade gun. The single fragment of a mainspring is rather amorphous, but a mid-19th Century date is reasonable. There is no necessary assumption that the excavated materials were actually merchandise at Ft. Pierre II—rather such firearms were in general circulation at the period and may well be of external origin.

II **Gun flints** (See Fig. 54)
 A—Square backed or Double-edged—
 The five examples are mottled grey-black in color, one is amber and quite translucent.
 Range of length—0.78"-1.10", Range of width—0.68"-0.88"

 B—Rounded ("gnawed")heel—
 Seventeen examples are taffy or amber in color; seven others are identical in shape, but have been subjected to such intense heat the the original character of the material is not discernible. Seven additional specimens are fragmentary, but probably fall with the "rounded heel" group.
 Range of Length—1.03"-1.33", Range of Width—0.99"-1.19"
 Remarks—many of the flints show evidence of extensive use and resharpening.

English flints have been conventionally distinguished from those of French origin by both form and material (color). The former are characteristically square cut with an opaque dark color preferred. French flints are amber or taffy colored, proportionately thinner and with rounded, retouched ("gnawed") heels. While such a distinction may not be entirely valid, these criteria as such indicate the presence of both varieties in the Ft. Pierre collection.

Gun flints were regularly graded in size, each suitable for use in a specific type of firearm. In actual practice, however, there seems to have been a reasonable variability in size. Although differences are nominal, there is little to indicate an exact correlation between named types (musket, rifle, pistol, etc.) and published dimension.[11] Manufacturing processes and the nature of the material made complete uniformity impossible. Flint sizes, in all probability, merely represent modes about which cluster many minor variations. The Ft. Pierre sample is quite variable; the length dimension of some examples has been altered by use and re-sharpening. Despite the lack of complete correspondence, the large "French" grouping (B) is of Musket size; the smaller group (A) seems to be of the Rifle category.[12]

Although Ft. Pierre II is a relatively late site, the substantial quantity of gun flints is not at all surprising. The flintlock ignition system was widely used by Indians; indeed, it seems to have been favored. Flints or flint-like silicates capable of striking fire were often available when percussion caps or cartridges were not. The continued demand for flintlock arms is reflected in the many trade specimens dated as late as the 1870's.

III Percussion Caps

A—Rifle or pistol caps—
Thick (mean: 0.011 in.), ribbed copper body, probably varnished, six intact. nine exploded.
Mean length—0.226", Mean internal diameter—0.175"
Remarks—size No. 12 or No. 13, usual for use with a sporting rifle. The thick-walled percussion caps of this sort are probably of English manufacture.

B—Musket Caps—
Copper, three with split flange ("Top Hat"), one ribbed, exploded.
Remarks—flanged specimens suggest typical military issue, but they were also widely used by civilians with surplus arms.

IV Bullets and Shot

A—Cylindro-conical—
39ST217-792: Item has flat base, ogive obliquely flattened, probably originally rounded, two shallow crimping grooves. this projectile has been fired (six wide grooves, ca. .005 deep, twist to the left), probably in a revolver.
Diameter—.421", Weight—225 grains
Remarks—a .44 WCF (44/40) 1875.

39ST217-134: Heeled bullet, flat base, rounded nose slightly deformed, rifling marks obscured.
Diameter—.224", Weight—24.1 grains
Remarks—.22 R.F., Short or Long. Probable date: such projectiles have been produced uninterruptedly since the late 1850's. The current specimen, however, seems to be recent.

B—Spherical—
39ST217-205 A: Poorly cast, incomplete "puddled" sprue, many knife marks over body.
Diameter—.461", Weight—126.4 grains

39ST217-205 B: No evident sprue, distinct planes around major circumference suggest that it was fired in a rifle or a pistol with a patch, thus obscuring the rifling marks. One face, perpendicular, is quite flattened. The surface of the compressed area is "crinkled", suggesting impact with the earth.
Mean Diameter—.400", Weight—75.2 grains

39ST217-1044A: No evident sprue, slightly deformed, probably fired with patch.
Mean Diameter—.534", Weight—214.8 grains

39ST217-1044 B: No sprue, slightly deformed but apparently un-fired, possibly "rolled" for truing.
Mean Diameter—.651", Weight—459.5 grains

39ST217-1044 C: No evident sprue, fired, one face flattened by im-pact, no other ballistic marks.
Mean Diameter—.525", Weight—197.0 grains

39ST217-1044 D: No evident sprue, fired, one face flattened by im-pact, no other ballistic marks.
Diameter—.524", Weight—205.7 grains

39ST217-1044 F: Cut sprue, fired, patch marks evident.
Mean Diameter—.525", Weight—209.0 grains

39ST217-1044 G: Irregularly cut sprue, no evidence of firing.
Mean Diameter—.301", Weight—78.5 grains

39ST217-136 A: Flattened spherical bullet.
Diameter—?, Weight—167.0 grains

39ST217-136 B: Small tit sprue, unfired.
Mean Diameter—.526", Weight—226.5 grains

39ST217-126 C: Badly corroded surface.
Diameter—.525", Weight—197.0 grains

39ST217-136 D: Flat cut sprue, cast in poorly fitting mould, fired, faint patch marks.
Mean Diameter—.471", Weight—167.0 grains

39ST217-136 E: Small tit sprue, unfired.
Diameter—.322", Weight—43.5 grains

39ST217-136 F: Roughly cut sprue, cast in irregular mould, un-fired.
Diameter—.372 X .341", Weight 57.0 grains

39ST217-136 G: Flat Cut sprue, unfired.
Diameter—.318", Weight—45.0 grains

39ST217-136 H: Flat cut sprue, unfired.
Mean Diameter—.327", Weight—46.0 grains

C—Shot—

	Diameter	American Standard Shot Size
39ST217-205 C:	.152 (2)	No. 2
	.127 (1)	No. 4 or 5
	.131 (1)	No. 4
	.123 (1)	No. 5
	.107 (1)	No. 6 or 7
39ST217-1361:	.262 (3)	No. 2 or 3 (Black) (Buck)
	.210-.220 (6)	TT-F
	.185-.198 (6)	BBB-T
	.157-.167 (4)	No. 1 or 2
	Small shot No. 7-9	

V Lead Bead

39ST217-1361: Probably originally a spherical bullet; surface badly cut and abraded, pierced or gouged hole paralleling long axis.
Dimensions—.364" X .313", Weight—52.0 grains

The two conical projectiles represent recent instrusions. While both are characterized by potentially long temporal ranges, they show little evidence of surface oxidation. Although this criterion is equivocal, a comparison with the physical condition of the other bullets in the collection suggests relative recency.

Of the total of sixteen spherical bullets, six (37½ percent) fall within a size range of .524-.526 inches. Most of the specimens are slightly deformed or "out of round", deriving from firing impact, or in some cases, possibly from battering in a carrying pouch. As a whole, a mean diameter of .525 is characteristic. Bullet weights are even more variable, resulting from variation in alloy, casting holes, and the loss of weight due to discharge and impact.

The .525 diameter bullet is the proper projectile for use in a wide range of .54 cal. U.S. martial arms current in the first half of the 19th

Century. The majority of the fired .525 bullets from Ft. Pierre II show no rifling marks despite other evidences of having been discharged. This probably indicates use in a smooth-bored firearm, perhaps a single shot martial pistol or a trade fusil. Two of the series seemed to have been used in rifles, one perhaps in a polygrooved bore such as the Hall's Model 1819 breechloader, although there is little evidence of its use on the frontier at the relatively late date of Ft. Pierre II. The other has been utilized with a patch. Although a number of arms could be indicated as possibilities, the Model 1841 or "Mississippi" Rifle seems to be the best choice since it was evidently widely distributed on the frontier, in large part in the hands of civilians.

Of the two larger projectiles, the .651 diameter example would have been suitable for use in a U.S. musket, calibre .69, particularly the Model 1842 or earlier. The .534 diameter, since it was probably fired with a patch, suggests use in a "plains rifle", or possibly a trade rifle, although the latter are little known.

The spherical bullets of smaller diameter are much more variable. The .372-471 diameters, some showing patch marks, indicate use in a rifle or single shot rifled pistol. Such a rifle would probably be of the "squirrel" or modified Kentucky type, that is, a small bore rifle suitable for the hunting of small game. The smaller projectiles, .301-.327, might well have been classified as shot, since they fall within the recognized size range of buckshot. However, the presence of a sprue shows that they were cast, not dropped. Cast shot, in the larger sizes, was often used, but does not seem to have been common at the date of Ft. Pierre II. It seems probable that at least the two largest specimens might have been intended for a .31 caliber revolver or pepper-box. The sample of small shot is varied as to size, but the many larger specimens would be particularly suitable for water fowling.

In total, the sample of firearms and related materials from Ft. Pierre II, although small, provides a confirmation of the firearms predictably present at such a spot. The day of the Mountain Man and the Fur Brigades was past. The trading "Fort", by the 1860's no longer served so much as an outfitting center, but as a wholesale-retail establishment of considerable stability. Arms were more important for trade exchange of subsistence hunting than for daily calls of defense.

---

[1] Smith, C.S. (1955) "An Analysis of the Firearms and Related Specimens from Like-A-Fishhook Village and Fort Berthold I", THE PLAINS ANTHROPOLOGIST, No. 4.

² Smith, G.H. (M.S.), "Excavation of Site of Fort Pierre II, Missouri Basin Project" RIVER BASIN SURVEYS, Smithsonian Institution.

³ Russell, Carl P. (1944) "The Trade Musket", MUZZLE BLASTS, Vol. 5, No. 10.
_____, (1957) GUNS ON THE EARLY FRONTIERS.
Ewers, Arthur J. (1956) "The Northwest Trade Gun", ALBERTA HISTORICAL REVIEW, Vol. 4, No. 2, pp. 1-7.
Hanson, Chas. E., Jr. (1955) THE NORTHWEST GUN.

⁴ ibid., p. 36.

⁵ ibid.

⁶ ibid.

⁷ ibid., p. 40.

⁸ ibid.

⁹ ibid.

¹⁰ ibid., p. 41.

¹¹ Archer, H.G., "The Oldest Industry In England", THE WIDE WORLD MAGAZINE, March, 1906, pp. 527-53.
Woodward, Arthur (1951) "Some Notes on Gunflints", MILITARY COLLECTOR AND HISTORIAN, Vol. III, No. 2, pp. 29-36. (Reprinted in this book).

¹² ibid., p. 36.

Chapter 9
THE TUSCARORA MUSEUM COLLECTIONS

The photographs and information constituting figures 55, 56, 57, 58 were received from Tom Pike, Director of the Tuscarora Museum, located approximately six miles west of Lisbon, Ohio. These excellent examples of 17th Century gun parts represent surface finds picked up along the old Tuscarora Trail over which the Iroquois passed in their war with the Illinois in 1680-1684. However, most of these gun parts were either lost or discarded forty to fifty years before that time. The probabilites are that most of them came from firearms gotten from Dutch traders and are, presumably, of Dutch origin.

Figure 55. Gun Parts.

Locks, top to bottom: A very early Dutch dog lock. Probably from a pistol, 4 1/2 inches long, 3/4 inch high back of the pan. Hammer is 2 5/8 inches high and made in two pieces forged together. No bridle on tumbler. Three sidescrews. Period 1620-1630. Early Dutch dog lockplate. Hole for dog catch. Plate, 5 1/8 inches x 15/16 inch. Two sidescrews. Period 1640. Dutch look, 5 5/8 inches x 1-1/16 inches. Square pan, 7/8 inch x 5/8 inch. Pan fastened by screw from outside. Tumbler has one notch. Sear acts laterally. Three sidescrews. Hammer made of two pieces, 2 5/8 inches high. Period 1630. Dutch lock 5 5/8 inches x 1-1/16 inches. Tumbler has two notches and regular type sear and spring. Tail of lock tapers for 1/2 inch. Plate shows flower engraving. Period 1670. Lockplate similar to above. Mainsprings range from 2 3/4 inches to 3 5/8 inches in length. The third and fourth are from very large locks. Gun barrel fragments measure 1 1/8, 13/16 and 1 inch in diameter. They are of .50, .59 and .75 caliber respectively. The upper fragment only is a breech section.

Information and photo courtesy Tuscarora Museum.

Figure 56. Gun flints and Bullets.

Top: Gun flints from campsites in the Ohio Valley. These are a mixed lot. The third and fifth flints in the top row, and the fourth and sixth in the bottom row are English, while the second and fifth in the bottom row are French. The first, third and seventh in the bottom row are Indian. The second in the first row appears to be a gunspall.

Bottom: The top row is composed of bullets of .70 and .72 caliber. The calibers of those in the bottom row are .75, .77, .80, .64, .72, .50, .47, .46. It is indeed interesting to find bullets of .50 caliber and less, but these may be rifle bullets of the late 18th Century.

Information and photo courtesy Tuscarora Museum.

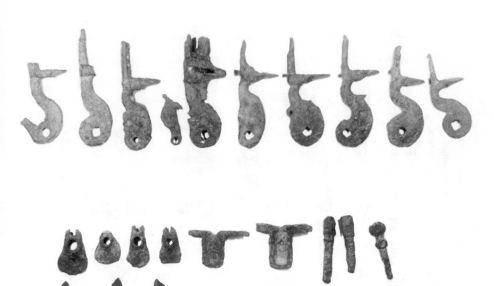

Figure 57. Miscellaneous Gun Parts.

Cocks, left to right:

1. Cock from early dog lock using lateral sear. Two piece cock, 2 1/2 inches high.
2. A two piece cock of the 1640-1660 period.
3. A 1640-1660 cock almost identically like "F", Figure 4.
4. Catch and dog lock cock, two piece, 3 1/2 inches high. Period 1640.
5. Another dog lock cock, but of one piece, 3 1/4 inches high. Period 1650.
6. This appears to be a ring type cock similar to No. 3, two piece, 3 1/4 inches high. Period 1660.
7. This is a cock typical to the last quarter of the 17th Century. One piece, 3 1/4 inches high. Period 1670.
8.& 9. Late 17th or early 18th Century type cocks. They are probably English. Upper vise jaws. Jaw No. 1 fits No. 6 cock, No. 2 fits No. 3, No. 3 fits No. 5, and No. 4 fits No. 7. The vise screws and pans are of the 1630-1660 period.

Information and photo courtesy Tuscarora Museum.

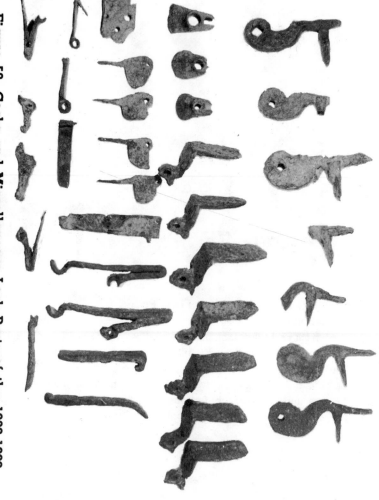

Figure 58. Cocks and Miscellaneous Lock Parts of the 1630-1660 Period.

Note that one of the mainsprings has collapsed from use. This was probably thrown away when replaced. The spring next to it appears to still have its original contour and may have been carried as a spare.

Information and photo courtesy Tuscarora Museum.

II
GUNFLINTS

Chapter 10
SOME NOTES ON GUNFLINTS
Arthur Woodward

It has been said that the knapping of flint is the oldest industry in Great Britain, and certainly after the introduction of flintlock firearms in the early part of the 17th Century, the making of gun flints became one of the most flourishing industries in that country. Before the days of flintlock firearms, thousands of years before Englishmen were wearing trousers, paleolithic and neolithic man was burrowing into the chalk strata of England after flint nodules from which to fashion his knives, spear heads and axes. The 17th Century Britons simply took over where their stone age ancestors had left off. The ancient workings were reopened, and even the prehistoric tools were copied.[1]

The town of Brandon in Suffolk County became the center of the gun flint making industry around 1686, and thence until 1835 the flint knappers of Brandon turned their entire output of flints into the government magazines. There were other towns near Brandon which also made flints, and in 1846-1850 the flint workers of Brandon shifted their scene of activity to Icklingham but continued to live in their own village. Flints were likewise produced at Savenham, Tuddenham and Mildenhall.[2]

The bulk of the flint used in the making of gun flints came from Lingheath Common about one to two miles from Brandon, southeast of the town. Three miles to the northeast of Brandon are ancient workings known as "Grime's Graves". H.G. Archer states that although Lingheath had been worked for around 2000 years it was not as old as Grime's Graves quarry. Permission to dig for flint at Lingheath was originally granted by the trustees of the town. Each digger mined his own flint and stored his "jags' or piles of nodules in sheds, or, if they were left in the open, he covered the freshly mined flint with grass and branches of trees to prevent the sun from reaching the stone and thereby changing its color. Later the nodules were dried by the fireside before delivering them to the knappers.[3]

The nodules occur in four or five layers of chalk, and pits were dug about 8 feet long, 4 feet wide and 6 feet deep as starting points. In this way, by steps, the digger continued on into the chalk bed and burrowed out for the flint nodules. The latter weighed from 25 to 200 pounds each. In some places, these chimney-like pits extended down for a depth of 40 feet or more, and when the digger struck a "floor" in the stratum he was mining, he burrowed out for the nodules.

The tools used in excavating the flint were a short iron crow bar and a steel tipped iron pick, fashioned in the shape of the deer antler pick used by the original flint workers in ancient times. A hollowed out piece of chalk with a candle in it provided a primitive miner's lamp.

The large chucks of flint, coated with a hard white layer of mineral, were delivered to the knappers who converted the blocks into flakes. The nodules were first "quartered". Archer said, "The art of quartering lies in breaking the stone so as to leave a more or less square edge to begin flaking from. Two sizes of hammers are used weighing three pounds and six pounds respectively. They are hexagonal in section and tapered to leave the face large."[4]

In beginning the knapping, a block of flint was placed upon a thick leather pad supported on the workman's knee. This was tapped with a heavy hammer to see if the flint was sound. If the coat was hard and the hammer rang, the stone was of good quality. If the hammer brought forth a dull sound and jumped, the flint was sure to be double coated and gray or mixed in color and therefore not considered of best grade. The stone was nearly always struck upon the natural, upper surface, because the bottom was softer and the hammer could not bite in as well.

Flaking was the most difficult part of the business. Many knappers were unable to flake properly. The knack lay in being able to strike the stone properly at the right angle and in the exact spot with an even force. Sir Francis H.S. Knowles, one of the most scientific students of the gun flint industry, presents the clearest picture yet given of one of these craftsmen:

"The knapper is seated on a low stool to the side of a circular bole formed of a section of a large tree trunk (elm or oak). The knapper sits with his left leg extended tangent to and touching the side of the bole, his right elbow closely set into his right groin and his wrist resting on his left thigh.

"The end of the knapping hammer is grasped in the fingers of the right hand with the thumb resting upon the flat surface of the haft to prevent the hammer turning in his hand when the blow is delivered.

"The knapping blow is given entirely by the wrist, the forearm being held quite still and pressed close to the body. For thin flakes the force required is little more than due to the weight of the hammer falling through an arc about six inches in length, but for a thick flake, a good sharp blow is necessary.

"The stake is set about four or five inches from the edge of the bole with its long edge at right angles to the long axis of the hammer and forearm.

"When there is no flake in position, the blow falls on the leather at the root of the stake and clears the upper edge of the stake by about half an inch.

"The flake to be cut into gun flints is held in the left hand with the bulbar surface uppermost and is pressed firmly on the edge of the stake making contact with the right hand side of the stake facing the knapper. The thumb is pressed in the bulbar side of the flake, while the fingers are pressed at the same time on the back of the stake and on the under side of the flake so as to secure a rigid contact.

"The striking edge of the knapping hammer is about one tenth of an inch thick and about 1¼ inches wide. When new, the head of the knapping hammer is about eight inches long and the edge is square, but when worn by use the edge becomes oblique, sloping down from left to right. From time to time this obliquity is removed by filing."[5]

Archer states that a knapper could tell at a glance how many, and what kind of flints each flake would make. A good flake would produce four flints, and a very good one would make five. Each knapper had his own peculiar style; which enabled him to tell his flints at a glance. An expert knapper could knock off flints blindfolded.[6]

Knowles remarks that:

"The French knappers (now extinct) used a hammer head in the form of a thin disc which made a point contact on the flake, but they were unable to produce the undercut fracture by means of a single blow. They produced the under cut by removing a series of small flakes or 'gnawed' edges and heels were sent to Brandon to be trimmed by the single blow, undercut fracture.

"From a technical standpoint, the undercut fractures on gun flints are of great interest. In normal flaking, the parent block bears the pit of the percussion or negative conchoid, while the flake which is detached bears the positive conchoid of bulbar swelling. In gun flints the 'knot' or mark of percussion which takes the form of a demi-cone is formed by the reaction of the stake and not by the hammer.

"When knapped, the end of the flake projects about half an inch beyond the edge of the stake and the left-hand corner of the hammer, when in action, is over the mid point of the width of the flake."[7]

Thomas Wilson, in his report on the manufacture of gun flints, states that the gun flints of commerce were divided into twenty-three classes according to the size and shape required for different arms. Usually, however, there were only about nine standard sizes of gun flints used, but it is to be understood that special locks might require specially sized flints.[8]

The number of flints produced by the individual workman varied according to the skill of the knapper. Archer remarked that a good worker could flake so fast that the sound of the blow and the falling flake hitting the tub were simultaneous. An expert knapper could knock off from 5,000 to 7,000 flakes per day, and a record was 63,000 flakes a week. This record was for flakes only. The finished flints took longer, but a good flint-maker could turn out between 2,000 and 3,000 flints daily or between 12,000 a 18,000 per week[9]

An author in the mid-19th Century describing the manufacture of Brandon flints said:

"The man (the "cracker") has before him three open casks into one of which he drops the larger flakes, into the second the flakes of less size and into the third the smallest flakes.

"Each cask goes to a separate workman called a *napper* who finishes them into flints, as musket flints, carbine flints, horse pistol flints, single barrel flints, double barrel flints and pistol flints. One cracker can keep three nappers employed."[10]

According to Wilson, the average weekly output of gun flints for twenty Brandon workmen was from 200,000 to 250,000. Flints sold at about one dollar per 1000.

The flint knappers used time candles in lieu of clocks to measure their working hours. Candles were divided into three parts by means of small flint flake wedges, each part between the flints burned for one hour. Chalk candlesticks of primitive form were also used.

The knapper reckoned his finished flints by the hundred. He picked them out, five at a time, with a nail and brushed them into a tin. He tallied each hundred by placing a spare flint at one side. The older workmen used strange, cabalistic signs in their tallying system, the meaning of which was forgotten, so long had they been in use. The flints were packed into tubs or sacks, carrying between 5,000 and 20,000, and the knappers sold their products *"per mille"*, using the French term which had been introduced into the country by French prisoners of war taken during the Marlborough campaign.[11]

From Brandon the flints were sent to Liverpool, Bristol, Birmingham and London for transhipment overseas. In the old days the British and foreign governments bid for the finest flints. Prior to the Crimean War, the largest order for gun flints came from the Turks, who ordered 11,000,000 of them for their forces.[12]

The color of gun flints seems to have been one of the criteria for judging their excellence, although in reality the color would seem to have but little bearing upon the quality of the stone. One English authority on shooting, Colonel Peter Hawker, writing in the early

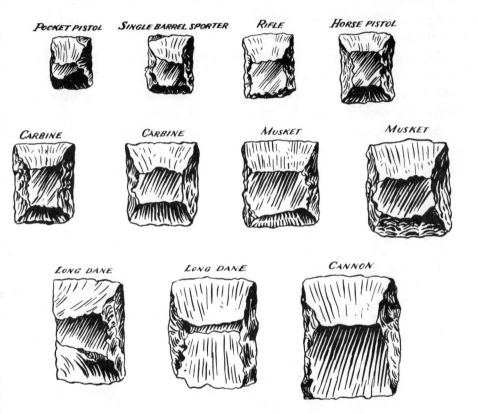

Figure 59. Flints made in Brandon by Mr. Herbert Edwards in 1948.
Collection of Arthur Woodward.

1820's said: "None are better than the most transparent of the common black flints. Great quantities (considered as good as any) come to London from Lord Cadogan's estate, at Brandon. They should be put in with the flat side upwards, stand well clear of the hammer (frizzen), and yet be long enough to throw it."[13]

In more recent years modern shooters of the flintlock pieces seem to favor light-colored flints. James E. Hicks states that, "Black flints were the poorest and were used only when the supply of others failed." Contemporary 18th and early 19th Century sources do not bear out Hicks' assertion.[14]

According to Archer, the natives in Africa regarded light colored or spotted flints as being inferior to the darker colored ones, hence it was a common trick of the trade to dip the light colored flints in a secret chemical preparation to darken the stone.

A contributor to the *Cyclopaedia or Universal Dictionary of Arts, Sciences and Literature,* London, 1819, devotes a number of paragraphs to gun flints, their manufacture, sizes, etc.:

"For a musquet one inch and five eights, for the length with a width of one inch and a quarter; the thickness at the back side one third of an inch, and the tapering to be rather sudden than gradual, something like the end of a chisel. Such flints fit well in the vice, being previously laid in a bed of thin sheet lead, or for want of it, in stout leather. The edge of a flint thus formed is far less subject to splinter than where the angle is more acute. It may perhaps be objected that a thin edge strikes fire better than a thick one, but that will be for only a few rounds; whereas the thicker edge resists better, and preserves an equable facility of scintillating for a long time.

"A carbine flint should be one inch and a quarter in length by one inch in width; that for a pistol, such as is used among our military, ought to be rather more than an inch in length by three quarters in width. In fixing them into the vise, great care should be taken that the left side may pass down clear of the barrel, which they would otherwise hack very much, and be themselves subject to splinter, while the cock itself might, by being unduly checked, be snapt at its neck.

"When Flints have a curve, they should always be so fixed in the vise as to give the curve a downward direction; since, in that way, they act more forcibly, and offer the greatest resistance. Straight flints, after being so far rounded as to yield no sparks, when their chamfered sides may have been uppermost, may be again rendered serviceable by being reversed, so as to bring their flat sides uppermost. Soaking flints in water restores them partially, probably by supplying them with hydrogen, but in a very small degree, and that not permanently. The best flints are such as, when acted upon by steel, produce strong, lasting corruscations which emit a sulphureous smell, and are sufficiently large to leave some little stain on tissue paper, or on fine lint. Such will not only be found to yield a certain fire, but to break up admirably under the hammer employed to reduce them to splinters, and to fit them for the soldier's use. On the contrary, however clear, black and firm a flint may appear, if its sparks are not vivid, and highly sulphureous, it ought to be at once thrown aside. The hardest flints are generally the best."

This same author also states that agates and carnelians, while hard, had been tried but proved to be too brittle. However, they would do in a pinch if no true flints were available. He also said that musket flints were packed 2000 in small casks called half barrels weighing 2^{qrs} 14 lbs., carbine flints, 3,000 to a cask, weight 2^{qrs} 10 lbs., while 4,000 pistol flints were packed in a cask, weight 2^{qrs} 15 lbs.

In 1837 Dr. James Mitchell visited Brandon, where he was informed the French no longer made gun flints and that the Brandon makers were the only ones in the world. About 70 or 80 men were employed. Apparently the French flint knappers hugged the secret of their methods close to their breasts. Tomlinson stated that . . . "Flint of the best quality adapted to the making of gun-flints, is comparatively rare in France as well as in England. Dolomieu states that where twenty beds of flint were found lying one above another, only one or two of these would afford good flint. On the banks of the Cher, flints were obtained by sinking shafts to the depths of 40 or 50 feet, from which horizontal galleries where driven through the one good stratum found."[15]

According to Clarke, French flints were first made regularly as a business in 1719, although flintlocks had been in vogue long before that date. During the 18th Century French flints from the Champagne and Picardy regions were considered too valuable for export. In general one might say that the French flints were of the honey or taffy colored types, with rounded heels, thinner and flatter than those of English manufacture. French flint nodules were more globular in form, the knobbed or branch flints were usually full of imperfections. Good nodules seldom weighed more than 20 pounds. When they weighed less than two pounds they were seldom worth working. The French flints had more of a greasy lustre, and the best ones were smooth and fine grained. It was said that the translucency of the flint of the best grade was such that a slice of it 1/50th of an inch thick, placed upon a print should be clear enough to read through. Flints manufactured in Germany, on the other hand, were made from agates and conglomerates and were less efficient and more expensive than either the French or English flints. There were other places in Europe where flints were made. In Albania for example, the chief flint knapping was done in Valona and in the village of Drasnovitza. Here, the flint work was different from either the British or the French, the flints being uniformly chipped on both faces.[16]

Ezekiel Baker, well known gun maker in England during the latter part of the 18th and early part of the 19th Centuries, became concerned over the variance in the sizes of gun flints. Said he, "The irregularity in size of flints, however, causes great inconvenience, particularly for muskets; and complaints have been frequently made, with great justice, as to the detriment under which the service lies from the want of a standard gauge. To obviate this evil I have adopted a gauge by which flints may be cut to one uniform size; and the plan has been so highly approved by the Honorable Board of Ordnance and the East India company, that they have gauges made for their use. The same gauge may be adapted to rifle guns, fusees, carbines and pistols, and indeed to every description of firearms; and must prove particularly advantageous where the jaws of the cocks are made right to receive them."[17] One only wishes that Ezekiel had gone a step further and illustrated his flint-sizing gauge.

Baker also emphasized the need of placing the flint in a proper position to strike against the frizzen. Failure to do so was one of the causes of misfires. If the cock and frizzen were not in the proper position, the flint was likely to strike too high on the face of he frizzen and the sparks would not fall into the pan. His remedy for striking too high or too low was this:

"If it strikes the hammer (frizzen) so high that the fire is dispersed, then lay double the lead or leather that the flint is fixed in under the flint against the cock, which will lower the fore part of the flint, and cause it to strike the hammer lower; if it strikes too low, double the lead or leather, as before mentioned, under the flint at the fore end of the under jaw of the cock, which will raise it to a proper position to fire. As the jaws of the cocks are not all of the same shape, a piece of paper or any soft substance, carefully placed under the flint at either end, as may be required, according to the foregoing directions, will fix it sufficiently firm. This remedy will be found useful in the flinting of all locks, as well as muskets, &c. as much depends on the flint being put in properly for the lock to fire true and well."[18]

On the other hand the same author points out that a piece might misfire when the flint was perfectly good and well set. This fault he attributed to the fact that the frizzen face of steel, being welded on, often became soft through frequent firing, and the flint cut through the casehardening. Thus the steel was destroyed, and the fire drawn from it by the flint was not as strong as it should be. Blunted flints striking such burned frizzen faces drew few or no sparks, and hence the pieces were practically useless until the frizzen faces were retempered.

Another cause of a misfire was the faulty flint itself. Some flints had hard spots in them which would neither nip nor break when the shooter tried to re-edge them, nor would these spots break out when the flint struck the face of the frizzen. The only remedy in this instance was either to discard the flint or break it down to secure a new edge entirely. The latter process sometimes made the flint too small for the jaws of the cock and hence useless.

In the United States, there were no centers for the manufacture of gun flints. There are various deposits of chert (which is not deemed a true flint) but none of these was used for making gun flints. Colonel John Trumbull of the American Army made this entry in his Orderly Book at Fort Ticonderoga, 10 November 1776, but whether he succeeded in obtaining the workmen he desired is not known.

"A vein of prodigious black Flint stone being discover'd upon Mt. Independence the Gen'l. desires the Commanding Officers of Regimts. will make inquiry if there are any Old Countreymen in any of their Corps, who understand the hammering of Gun Flints, upon such a person or persons found, he or they, are to be sent to the Genl. at Head Quarters."[19]

There are hundreds of gun flints in the museum at Fort Ticonderoga. The majority of them are light in color ranging from gray to waxy brown. Most of them have the rounded, gnawed heels and are thin and flat. Surprisingly few of the black, squared Brandon type flints are in the collection. There are some flints which might be of local manufacture, but since it was not possible to visit the site of the "vein of prodigious black Flint stone" on Mt. Independence, just across the water from the fort, it could not be determined whether the flints were made there or elsewhere. Hence, it is believed most of the flints in the museum are of French origin.

Occasionally, on Indian camp sites, particularly in Kansas, gun flints, chipped out of old arrow or spear heads, have been found. These are easily recognizable by their shape and workmanship. They are thin, square, and chipped all over.

The old lists of trade goods are filled with requests for thousands of gun flints. One order, for example, calls for "4,000 black flints for trading guns" and "1,000 ditto for Fowling Pieces". Other orders were "2000 common flints" and "300 best flints". Twelve flints was the price paid for one pound of leather in trade in Georgia in 1765, and in 1785, one half dozen flints sold for seven pence in the same region.[20]

These flints are today scattered over the face of the United States and Canada. Every year farmers turn them out of the ground, and archaeologists find them in Indian burial and camp sites. Even after percussion locks were invented, gun flints continued to be manufactured at Brandon. Flints for use as strike-a-lights were also made and sold in those countries where matches were at a premium. In Mexico particularly among the poorer classes in the states of Durango and Zecatecas, flint and steel were used as late as the early '50s. The flints in these places were chunks of local rock which give forth excellent showers of sparks when struck with the hand forged steels or *lesabones* (dialectically called *islabones* or *'slabones.*)[21]

After World War I the art of flint knapping at Brandon went into a sudden decline. Orders for gun flints and strike-a-lights, even in the most backward areas of the world had declined to such a low point that there was no longer any incentive to continue the craft. There was a period when there were no knappers at work. However, within the past twenty-five or so years several knappers have resumed work as a part time occupation. They send some flints to Africa, but the greatest demand is from the United States where the devotees of the flintlock are calling for flints from Brandon. Judging by flints received from England, manufactured in 1949, the skill of the apprentice knappers is increasing. A very good set of flints, made during the 1880's, is also to be seen in the collections of the Davenport Public Museum, Davenport, Iowa.[22]

In studying the accompanying chart of flint sizes, it will be noted that although there are minor variations in size within the different categories, still, the flints average up fairly evenly. There are other collections of gun flints in the United States aside from those used in the chart. One in the Museum of the American Indian, Heye Foundation, New York City, contains around 25 flints which came from the stock of a trading post at Butte des Morts, Wisconsin. These are a mixed lot, some are thin, flat, of light colored flint, with round gnawed heels; others are square and black. At least four of these flints appear to be of native American manufacture. There are 91 gun flints in a collection housed in the Wisconsin State Historical Society, Madison, Wisconsin, which vary considerably in size and shape. Some of these flints are quite thick and crude and were apparently knapped out of the rind of the flint nodules. Only seven of this batch are square cut. Judging by the dimensions of both the Heye collection and those in the Wisconsin Historical Society, the majority of these flints were for rifle and musket with perhaps a few horse pistol flints scattered through the lot.

Chart of Gun Flints.

Chart based on specimens in the collections of the author and the Davenport Public Museum as well as data from Archer's article.

	Davenport Coll.	Author's Coll.	Archer
		1 1/2"x1"	1 3/4"x1"
Long Dane Used with lengthy Arab gun)	none	1 1/2"x1 1/4"	
Musket	1 1/2"x1 1/2" 1 1/2"x1 3/16"	1 1/4"x1 5/8" 1 1/8"x1 1/4"	1 3/8"x1 1/4"'
Carbine	none	1 1/8"x1" 1 1/8"x7/8"	1 1/4"x1"
Horse Pistol	none	1"x3/4"	1"x1"
Pocket Pistol	9/16"x1/2" 3/4"x1/2"	11/16"x5/16"	5/8"x1/2"
Single (single barrelled sporting gun)	none	7/8"x3/4"	7/8"x7/8"
Fowling Piece	1 1/8"x5/16" 1 1/8"x1"	none	1 3/8"x1 3/8"
Rifle	none	none	7/8"x7/8"
Cannon	2 1/2"x2 1/4"	1 3/4"x1 1/2"	none
Old Tower Flints (musket)	1 1/2"x1 3/16" 1 1/2"x1 1/2"	none	none
Modern Musket	1 1/4"x15/16"	none	none
Flints for African Trade	1 5/16"x1 1/16"		
Strike-A-Light	2 1/8"x1 1/2"	1 7/16"x1 1/4"	none

1. Archer, H.G., "The Oldest Industry in England," THE WIDE WORLD MAGAZNE, March, 1906, pp. 527-533. See also Archer, "Oldest British Industry," Sunday magazine section, Los Angeles TIMES, 28 May 1905.

2. Clarke, Rainbird, "The Flint Knapping Industry at Brandon," ANTIQUITY, March, 1935, page 43.

3. Archer, H.G. (1906), "The Oldest Industry in England," THE WIDE WORLD MAGAZINE, March pp. 527-533.

4. Archer (1906), "The Oldest Industry in England," pp. 527-533.

5. Knowles, Sir Francis H.S. and Alfred S. Barnes, "Manufacture of Gunflints", ANTIQUITY, Vol. XI, No. 42 (June 1937), pp. 201-207.

6. Archer (1906), "The Oldest Industry in England", pp. 527-533.

7. Knowles (1937), "Manufacture of Gunflints", ANTIQUITY, Vol. XI, No. 42, p. 207.

8. Wilson, Thomas, "Arrowpoints, Spearheads and Knives", REPORT of the United States National Museum, Washington, 1897, pp. 861-864.

9. Archer (1906), "The Oldest Industry in England", pp., 527-533.

10. Tomlinson, Charles (1852), CYCLOPAEDIA OF USEFUL ARTS AND MANUFACTURES, 2 vols., London, p. 690, Vols. 1.

11. Archer (1906), "The Oldest Industry in England", pp. 527-533.

12. Ibid.

13. Hawker, Lt. Col. Peter, INSTRUCTIONS TO YOUNG SPORTSMEN, 4th edition, London, 1 8 2 5 ,
p. 98.

14. Hicks, Maj. James E., "U.S. Military Shoulder Arms, 1795-1935: The Smooth Bore Flintlock as a Military Arm," JOURNAL of the American Military History Foundation, I, no. 1, (Spring 1937), p. 23.

15. Tomlinson (1852), CYCLOPAEDIA OF USEFUL ARTS AND MANUFACTURES. 2 Vols., London.

16. Clarke, "Flint Knapping," p. 51. Tomlinson (1852), CYCLOPAEDIA OF USEFUL ARTS AND MANUFACTURES. 2 Vols., London, Arthur J. Evans, "On the Flint Knappers' Art in Albania," JOURNAL of the Anthropological Institute of Great Britain and Ireland, XVI, (1887), pp. 65-68.

17. Baker Ezekiel, REMARKS ON RIFLE GUNS, London, 1835, reprint edition, Huntington, West Virginia, n.d., pp. 35, 36.

18. Ibid., pp. 34, 35.

19. Trumbull, Col. John, ORDERLY BOOK, BULLETIN of Fort Ticonderoga Museum, III, No. 3 (January 1934), p. 156.

20. COLONIAL RECORDS OF GEORGIA, XXVIII, pt. 2, 106, 107, 271, 272, Galphinton Trading Post accounts, 12 October 1785-21 December 1787, Georgia Department of Archives and History, Atlanta, Georgia.

21. Observations made by author in Durango and Zacatecas, Mexico, October 1950.

22. Harvey, William, "Britain's Oldest Industry," THE RIFLEMAN, Summer 1947, pp. 25, 28. Personal correspondence with Geoffrey Turner, University Museum, Oxford, England.

[Chapter 11]
18th Century Manufacture of French Gun Flints
by
Carlyle S. Smith

The translation of the following two works is offered as information on French gun flints for use in identifying the European sources of trade goods found in aboriginal sites in the New World. It serves as a starting point in the pursuit of data from other sources on gun flints.

In 1953 G. Hubert Smith of the Missouri Basin Project, Smithsonian Institution, called to my attention the existence of the data on the manufacture of gun flints in France. Franklin Fenenga, University of Nebraska, had found a reference to the work of Dolomieu in his perusal of an old American encyclopedia (Cutbush, 1814) which contains an article on flint and flint working. G.H. Smith was successful in obtaining a copy of Volume 6 of the *JOURNAL DES MINES*, published in the Year 5 of the Republic Calendar, on interlibrary loan from Iowa State University. Photographic copies of the text and the engraving were made in the laboratory of the Missouri Basin Project and turned over to me. The pages include an article by Gillet-Laumont in addition to the one by Dolomieu.

The first article, by Citizen Dolomieu (1797), covers not only the methods of manufacture of gun flints in France at that time but also the nature of the flint itself. The second, by Gillet-Laumont (1797), contains abstracts of reports by Citizen Salivet (MS.) and Citizen Tonnelier (MS.) on the same subject, but with additional data on mining techniques.

With the aid of the Reference Department of the University of Kansas Library it was determined that "Citizen Dolomieu" was one Deodat Guy Silvain Tancrede, Gratet de Dolomieu, a renowned French mineralogist and vulcanist who lived from 1750 to 1801. The mineral *dolomite* was

147

named after him. "Citizen Salivet" was Louis George Isaac Salivet, 1737 to 1805, who was a public prosecutor for the Revolutionary Tribunal during the days of the extensive use of the guillotine for purposes of political liquidation. Later, he was chief of one of the bureaus of the First Republic concerned with small arms. He also wrote under the pseudonym of *Bergeron.* The full name of Gillet-Laumont was Francois Pierre Nicolas Gillet de Laumont. His obituary was published in 1816. The footnote at the end of Dolomieu's report is signed *Coquebert.* This individual was the Baron Charles Etienne Coquebert de Montbret, 1755 to 1831, who was the editor of the *JOURNAL DES MINES* from 1793 to 1795, the probable period in which the paper was submitted for publication. He was also a mineralogist, physician, and author. No data on Tonnelier could be found.

The maps of Cassini, referred to in both papers, are those submitted to the National Assembly in 1793 by Jacques Dominique, Compre de Cassini, 1747 to 1845. An outline map of France (Fig. 60) has been added on which the localities bearing the names of departments are encircled. The old French provinces referred to in the texts are indicated along with the locations of Paris and Troyes.

A literal translation of the paper by Gillet-Laumont was prepared by David Agee Norr. After the final copy of the translation of both papers was completed, G.H. Smith furnished a copy of an independent translation made by him. It was helpful to compare the renditions of the more difficult passages and thus provide smoother translations of them. In many instances it has been necessary to alter the style of the original, but this was done only for the purposes of clarity.

It has been necessary, in some cases, to alter the terminology for the English-speaking reader. The flintworkers term *nodule* is the same as the ordinary French word *caillou,* which means *pebble.* Dolomieu comments on this and uses the word *caillou* in referring to a *nodule.* In the translation the term *nodule* is used after Dolomieu's discussion of the term. Dolomieu's *silex pyromaque* means *fire-yielding flint.* This is freely translated as *fire-flint.* Measurements are given first as the authors present them and a second time in the modern form if the situation seems to warrant it.

The constituents of flint are all stable oxides, predominantly silicon dioxide, not subject to further alteration, other than the loss of water, by heat generated through friction or collision. Dolomieu must have

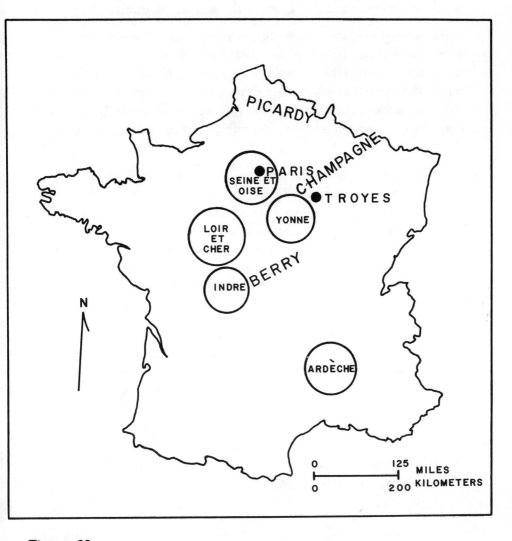

Figure 60.
Map of France showing the locations of flint-working localities (encircled); the provinces of Berry, Champagne, and Picardy; the cities of Paris and Troyes.

been influenced by the fire-yielding properties of pyrite (iron disulphide) in his attempts to discover some constituent in flint which might produce the sparks. When pyrite is struck by a piece of steel, or any very hard substance such as flint itself, sparks are thrown off. This is the mineral used in the past, in the wheellock gun.

As Gillet-Laumont points out, when flint strikes a piece of hard steel, particles of free iron are dislodged. The friction generated in this process causes the particles to become so hot that they oxidize, or burn, and appear as sparks. My experiments indicate that when flint is struck against ordinary iron a gouging action takes place and insufficient heat is generated to ignite any particles of iron that might be dislodged.

In seeking differences in specific gravity between flint and quartz, Dolomieu was handicapped by the crude methods available at the time. The specific gravity of quartz is 2.6, the same as Dolomieu computed for his fire flint from the banks of the Cher. The difference of .01 less for the fire flint from near Rochequyon does not appear to represent a significant difference. One might expect flint, with all its impurities, to have a specific gravity somewhat different from, more likely less than, pure quartz.

Colonel Berkeley R. Lewis discusses gun flints in his study of U.S. Army small arms and ammunition and finds that Congress authorized the employment of persons to make flints in 1776, but it does not appear that any flints were ever manufactured on this side of the Atlantic for our armed forces. In drawing upon a secondary source Lewis errs in identifying British flints as yellow and American as black. He quotes, as follows, the entire section on gun flints from the *ORDNANCE MANUAL* of the U.S. Army, 3rd edition published in 1849. (All measurements are in inches):

"*Flints*—The best flints are translucent, with a smooth surface, of a uniform light yellow or brown color, and slightly conchoidal fracture. They are generally obtained from England or France.

"The parts of flint are: the *edge* or *bevel*, the *back*, the *sides*, the *face*, slightly convex, and the *bed*, or lower face, slightly concave; in using the flint, the bevel is placed uppermost. There are three sizes for military service; *musket*, *rifle*, and *pistol* flints. A good musket flint will last for more than 50 fires. Flints are issued to the troops in the proportion of 1 flint to 20 rounds.

	Musket Min.-Max.		Rifle Min.-Max.		Pistol Min.-Max.	
Dimensions						
Whole length	1.20	1.50	0.97	1.20	0.93	1.10
Width	1.08	1.13	0.79	0.88	0.83	0.92
Thickness at back	0.26	0.33	0.20	0.29	0.21	0.27
Length of bevel	0.39	0.55	0.41	0.71	0.30	0.42

"The rifle and the musketoon take the same flint. In the inspection of flints, first verify their dimensions with the gauge, giving the maximum and minimum dimensions; see that the bevel is free from spots and irregularities of surface, that the face and bed are nearly parallel, and have not too great a curvature."[2]

In the above extract it is stated that the bevel is placed uppermost in the cock of the gun. While this may have been prescribed procedure in the U.S. Army it was a far from universal practice. I have found that flints often work better with the bevel down.

A blond French flint is seen clamped, bevel down, in the jaws of the cock of Model 1777 French military musket (Fig. 61) from my collection. A piece of leather is used to pad the flint. The lock of this piece is marked *Mre Rle de Tulle* which stands for *Manufacture Royale de Tulle,* a government armory in the city of Tulle. The musket was made from 1777 throughout the period of the First Republic and First Empire with only minor modifications.

A sample of 211 gun flints, from old U.S. Army stores, was purchased from Francis Bannerman Sons for study.[3] Of these, 180 are of blond colored flint and exhibit the same manufacturing techniques described by the French writers (Fig. 62). Thirty gun flints are of black flint (examples of some of these are shown in Fig. 62, a-k) and, with five exceptions (four of which are shown in Fig. 63, l-o), exhibit the characteristics attributed to English gun flints by Woodward (pp. 135-146). One unidentifiable flint is brownish in color (Fig. 63, k) and manufactured by a technique similar to that used in making the five unusual black flints.

A sample of newly manufactured English flints from the still active work shops at Brandon was purchased from Turner Kirkland, Dixie Gun Works, Union City, Tennessee, for comparative study (Fig. 63, q-t). A certain amount of decadence in manufacturing techniques is evident in comparison with many of the black flints in the Bannerman sample.

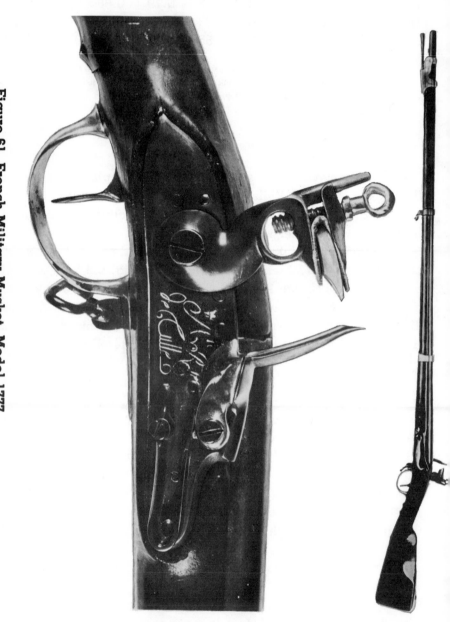

Figure 61. French Military Musket, Model 1777.
Left, full length view; right, enlarged view of the lock, showing a flint in place in the cock, padded with leather. Lock marked Mre Rle/de Tulle.

Figure 62. French Gun flints.
a-h, musket flints; l-p, rifle flints; q-t, pistol flints. All are classifiable as blond in color.

The 180 gun flints identifiable as French in the Bannerman sample are all classifiable as blond in terms of the predominance of that color (Fig. 62, a-t). Typical specimens are translucent and have opaque white inclusions. Some display reddish strains. Others have gray areas. Three flints are multi-colored with blond hue predominating (Fig. 62, g, t). One is entirely opaque and mostly yellowish in color (Fig. 62, h).

The blond French flints display secondary chipping along the sides and around the back. This results in a rounded back and a "gnawed" appearance in contrast with the smooth planes that resulted from the primary chipping. The black English flints in the Bannerman and Kirkland samples display little or no secondary chipping along the sides and across the back. The backs are square and each flint appears to owe its form almost entirely to primary flake scars similar to those on French flints. The gun flint illustrated in Dolomieu's Plate (Fig. 65, pg. 170) may have been engraved in a somehwat stylized manner because the back is almost as square as that of an English flint.

Among the 30 black flints in the Bannerman sample are five that display pronounced bulbs of percussion in the area known as the bed (Fig. 63, l-o). The entire surface from the back to the sharp edge of the area known as the bevel is a smooth convex surface. The one unidentified brown flint (Fig. 63, p) is similar in this respect. No data could be found on just how these flints were made. It seems likely that the convex flints were made from flakes which broke off the nodule just below the spot hit by the hammer. Such flakes often must have been long enough to be fashioned into single gun flints. If this interpretation is correct a few of them may have been made at nearly every work shop. It is worthy of note, however, that I have not seen any blond flints made in this way. Gray flints of this form have been picked up on the surface in South Dakota and two are in the collections from the Kansas Monument site in Republic County, Kansas[4].

In Table I p. 156, the measurements of the 180 blond flints from Bannerman are compared with the U.S. Army specifications which have been converted to millimeters. In Table 2 p. 157 the measurements of the other 31 flints from Bannerman are set forth. Musket flints are the largest. Rifle flints are medium in size and pistol flints are the smallest (Figs. 62 and 63). It should be noted that these are military designations. Military flintlocks are larger than those made for civilian

Figure 63. English Gun flints.
a-d, l, m, q, musket flints; e-h, n-p, r, rifle flints; i-k, s, t, pistol flints. a-k, old flat black flints; l-o, old convex black flints; p, unidentified, French or English, old convex flint; q-t, modern English flat flints, grading from gray to black in color.

firearms. Most musket flints are too large for firearms designed for hunting. Rifle and pistol flints might serve in civilian rifles and fowling pieces. Some rifles and pistols would require flints smaller than those designated as "pistol" by the military. Many guns made for the Indian trade utilized old musket locks which would accommodate the large musket flint, however.

It is noteworthy that the black English flints are characteristically narrower than the blond French flints. The minimum and maximum lengths in the samples often fall short of those set forth for the inspection flints. In many instances this is because some of the flints have had some use in a lock and have the sharp edge of the bevel worn off. Other discrepancies in dimensions are attributable to a lack of careful inspection on the part of the Ordnance Department of the U.S. Army at the time the flints were imported.

TABLE 1. Measurements of a sample of 180 blond gun flints from Francis Bannerman Sons compared with the minimum and maximum dimensions used in the inspection of gun flints for the U.S. Army in 1849.

	Bannerman Blond Gun flints		U.S. Army Specifications
	Range in mm.	Mean	Converted to millimeters
MUSKET SIZE:			
Whole length	27-35	31	30.5-38.1
Width	24-31	28	27.5-28.7
Thickness	5-11	8	6.6-8.4
Length of the bevel	7-24	12	9.9-13.9
Length of the bed	8-20	14	- - - -
Number in sample:	63		
RIFLE SIZE:			
Whole length	25-29	26	24.9-30.5
Width	20-25	22	20.3-22.4
Thickness	4-9	6	5.1-7.4
Length of the bevel	7-14	10	10.4-18.0
Length of the bed	7-18	14	- - - -
Number in sample:	62		

| | Bannerman Blond Gun flints | | U.S. Army Specifications |
	Range in mm.	Mean	Converted to millimeters
PISTOL SIZE:			
Whole length	21-26	24	23.6-27.7
Width	18-22	20	21.3-23.3
Thickness	5-9	6	5.3-6.9
Length of the bevel	5-13	10	7.6-10.9
Length of the bed	5-16	10	- - - -
Number in sample:	55		

TABLE 2. Measurements of a sample of 31 brown and black gun flints from Francis Bannerman Sons.

| | Bannerman Brown Convex Flints | Bannerman Black Flat Flints | | Bannerman Black Convex Flints |
	Size in mm.	Range in mm.	Mean	Range in mm.
MUSKET SIZE:				
Whole length	—	28-30	29	28-30
Width	—	24-25	24	24
Thickness	—	6-9	8	7-10
Length of the bevel	—	9-16	13	21-27
Length of the bed	—	4-15	9	0
Number in sample:	0	6		2
RIFLE SIZE:				
Whole length	27	25-28	27	27-28
Width	26	21-24	22	21-22
Thickness	6	5-7	6	6-8
Length of the bevel	22	9-16	13	24-27
Length of the bed	0	0-14	8	0
Number in sample:	1	16		3

	Bannerman Brown Convex Flint	Bannerman Black Flat Flints		Bannerman Black Convex Flint
	Size in mm.	Range in mm.	Mean	Range in mm.
PISTOL SIZE:				
Whole length	—	23-24	———	———
Width	—	18-20	———	———
Thickness	—	5-8	———	———
Length of the bevel	—	8-14	———	———
Length of the bed	—	0-13	———	———
Number in sample:	0	3	———	0

Since the above was written I have visited France and collected samples of flint from sites in the vicinity of Meusnes, Coufy, Lye, and Cerilly. Black flint is present in small amounts among the flakes at workshop sites near Meusnes and among the flints left over from the stock of the last dealer in gun flints and strike-a-lights, Marcel Plat of Villentrois (Indre). In the collection, now in the possession of the son, Roger Plat, he found a few black gun flints, some with rounded backs and some with squared backs. A few of the blond flints had squared backs. The industry lasted into the 1920's. It is said that the last shipments were made to Chile. Attempts will be made to determine if it is possible to distinguish black French flint from black English flint by chemical analysis, or other means.

1. Lewis, Berkeley R. (1956) "Small Arms and Ammunition In The United States Service," SMITHSONIAN INSTITUTION MISCELLANEOUS COLLECTIONS, Vol. 129, pp. 159-160.
   _____, Personal communication.
2. ORDNANCE MANUAL, U.S. Army (1849), 3rd Ed.
3. Bannerman, Fracis, et al, (1955) CATALOG OF MILITARY GOODS.
4. Smith, Carlyle S. (1950) "European Trade Material From the Kansas Monument Site", PLAINS ARCHAEOLOGICAL CONFERENCE NEWS LETTERS, Vol. 3, No. 2, p. 2. Hamilton, T.M. (1960) INDIAN TRADE GUNS, 1st Ed., p. 79.

MEMOIRE

Sur l'art de tailler les pierres à fusil (silex
.pyromaque) ;

Par le C.en DOLOMIEU, en l'an 5.

L'ART de faire des pierres à fusil, concentré
depuis long-temps dans un petit espace situé sur
deux départemens voisins, celui de Loir - Cher
et celui de l'Indre, exercé presque exclusive-
ment par les habitans de quatre communes dont
le territoire contient en grande abondance la ma-
tière sur laquelle ils emploient leur industrie, ne
donnant qu'un produit peu lucratif comme spé-
culation de commerce, quoique très - nécessaire,
comme moyen de défense, pour l'usage de l'arme
à laquelle il s'adapte ; cet art, dis-je, est très-peu
connu : car peu d'observateurs ont été à portée
d'en examiner les procédés, et je ne crois pas
qu'aucune description en ait encore publié les
détails. C'est en vain que j'ai recherché sur cet
objet quelques notions dans les ouvrages de miné-
ralogie ; c'est en vain que j'ai consulté ce qui a été
écrit sur les arts et métiers ; l'Encyclopédie elle-
même ne dit rien des procédés de cette taille, et
elle se contente de consacrer un préjugé ridicule,
déjà consigné dans les Mémoires de l'académie
des sciences, année 1738 : en parlant des silex
qui servent à la fabrication des pierres à fusil, il
y est dit « qu'ils ne manquent jamais dans les lieux
» où on les exploite, parce que dès qu'une car-
» rière est vide, on la ferme, et plusieurs années

*Préjugé su
la reproduc-
tion du silex.*

Figure 64. Title page of article by Dolomieu.

159

[Chapter 12]
The Art of Making Gun Flint
by Citizen Dolomieu
in the Year 5 [1796-1797]
Tranlated by Carlyle S. Smith

The art of making gun flints has been centered for a long time within a restricted area in the two neighboring departments of Loir-et-Cher and Indre. It is carried on almost exclusively by the inhabitants of four communes where the material which they work occurs in abundance. While the sale of the product is only slightly lucrative as a business venture, it is very necessary as a means of defense, using the weapon to which it is adapted. This art, I say, is little known. Few observers have examined the processes and I know of no detailed published description. I have searched in vain in the works of mineralogy and in what has been written on the arts and trades. The *ENCYCLOPEDIE* itself says nothing of the processes of manufacture and is content to accept a ridiculous apriori judgment derived from an article in the *MEMOIRES DE L'ACADEMIE DES SCIENCES* of 1738. In speaking of the flint which serves in the making of gun flints it is said 'that they are never lacking in places where they work because as soon as a pit is empty they close it. Several years afterwards they find gun flints as before.' See *ENCYCLOPEDIE ALPHABETIQUE*, article entitled, *"Pierre a fusil"*; signed D.J., and *MEMOIRES DE L'ACADEMIE DES SCIENCES, HISTOIR*, page 28, 1738.

The art of fashioning gun flints has remained for the most part among those problems treated by naturalists. In foreign countries many questions have been put to me on the subject, but I had not ever had sufficient knowledge of all the processes and had been hard put to explain that the material was not soft at the time it is worked in order for it to take the exact form desired. It could only be concluded that the flints were made without cutting tools because their low price would preclude the use of the wheel or the grindstone.

This art, extremely simple in its processes, carried on with a very small number of tools, requiring but a very short apprenticeship and an equally small amount of effort, is of interest in its own right. It achieves by a single blow forms as exact, facets as smooth, lines as straight, and angles as sharp as if the stone had been worked on a lapidary's wheel. Five or six little hammer blows and a minute of time suffice to obtain the same degree of perfection that would result from more than an hour of work if the cutters rubbed the material against harder substances or abraded it with emery. The result is that one pays a *denier* for one gun flint when it leaves the hands of the worker. This same flint would cost, of necessity, fifty times as much if it were fashioned by any other process.

I shall examine the substances upon which this art is practiced, including the tools used and the processes whereby the gun flints are fashioned, which best suits them to the use to which they are put, to the best of my ability.

SUBSTANCES USED FOR MAKING GUN FLINTS

In general, stones of all sorts might serve as gun flints, or as strike-a-lights if they could produce a good spark in striking against steel, if they could be fashioned easily into the proper form to fit the lock of a gun, and if they were not expensive. All such stones would be of some value, but one kind would be chosen from among them on the basis of its ability to yield more sparks with a minimum of shock in order to light powder. Such a stone should also mar the steel against which it strikes the least. These factors favor the stones classed as flints as opposed to those classed as quartose, which soon destroy the surface of the battery [frizzen] of the gun in which they are used. True flints have an additional advantage over others because it is easier to break them into fragments of the desired form and dimensions. It is among the flinty stones that the gun flint makers have found the substance truly appropriate for the exercise of their skill. Among the numerous varieties of stones of this kind there is but one that can be worked easily with a hammer. The agates and chalcedonies, of which gun flints are also made, are alterable into useful forms only through the use of the grindstone.

The gun flint makers call the stone that they use a "pebble' [*caillou*] and call themselves 'pebblers' [*caillouteurs*]. This work, which means to them the best stone and which is used elsewhere in France to mean only a rounded and isolated stone of any kind, has become the one used by many French naturalists to designate flints. This is, perhaps because most of the isolated stones in the vicinity of Paris, and of other chalky regions, are of this kind.

The nodule used by the workers in gun flints appears to be of the kind of flint that the naturalists have named *silex gregarius, silex ignarius, silex cretaceus, silex vulgaris, silex vagus,* the *Feuerstein* of the Germans, etc. All of the flints designated as plain, because they lack the brilliance and beauty of chalcedony and agate, are found scattered in the fields and seem to have been detached accidentally from their places of origin. All of the flints imbedded in chalk are not suitable for making gun flints. This is equally true of the flint which occurs in certain other places. This means that the nodule appropriate for the manufacture of gun flints is not common in nature. Many countries lack it entirely. It may also mean that France alone possesses the variety of flint needed for the easy manufacture of gun flints. It is incredible that the art of making gun flints should remain a mystery to other nations who do not manufacture them at all in spite of the fact that they make great use of them. The method of manufacture is so simple that they would have learned it soon if the substance was available to them. This may be the true reason for their lack of gun flints of their own manufacture.

In describing the variety of flint which serves best to make gun flints I have assigned the name of *silex pyromachus,* fire-yielding flint, which expresses its use and which I have preferred to *silex sclopetarius,* missil-thrower-flint, which appears to me to be less appropriate. Neither one nor the other of these terms is new. The old mineralogists have already used them.

SILEX PYROMACHUS, FIRE-YIELDING FLINT
METHODICAL DESCRIPTION
Exterior Characteristics

Exterior appearance. Fire flints are always covered with a white coating from 1 to 2 lines [about 1/12 to 1/6 in.], or more in thickness when they leave the quarry. The crust has an earthy appearance, is limey, and of loose consistency. It is much softer and weighs less than the flint it covers.

Exterior form. The material for good gun flints has a somewhat convex surface, or one which approaches a globular form. The very irregular flint nodules of bizarre forms are full of imperfections.

Volume. The best flints are found in the largest masses. The good nodules rarely exceed 20 pounds in weight and must not weigh less than one or two pounds.

Interior appearance. The interior of fire flint has a greasy appearance. It is a little glossy and has a grain that is so fine that it is imperceptible.

Color. In good fire flint the color may vary from honey yellow to blackish brown.

Note. The different shades in the masses of flint have no effect on their ability to serve as gun flints, rather it is the uniformity of their color when reduced to thin pieces. The nodules from the departments of Loir-et-Cher and Indre are yellowish. Those from the limestone hills which border the Seine are brownish. Both kinds when reduced to powder, are perfectly white.

Transparency. Flint ought to have a kind of greasy and uniform semi-transparency that permits the distinguishing of writing under a piece one quarter of a line [about 1/48 in.] in thickness.

Fracture. Fire flint ought to have a smooth fracture throughout. The surface should be very slightly conchoidal, *i.e.,* convex or concave. This kind of fracture is one of the properties of this variety of flint because it is to this that it owes the property of being convertible into gun flints.

Note. It is by these exterior characteristics that the workers recognize the stones appropriate to their work. It is by these that they judge their degree of perfection. They call those possessing all of the qualities *pure nodules* and those whose imperfections interfere with their fracture *grainy,* or *unmanageable, nodules.* They compare the part of the mass of flint which has a translucency and a uniform color, with the part of lard fat for which they use the word *couenne* [meaning 'rind' in modern French; the specialized meaning here is different]. They say that a given nodule has more or less *couenne* and that all is not *couenne* in a nodule. They say that the *couenne* of the upper part of a nodule is always better than that of the lower.

The nodules of fire flint are regarded as imperfect, or grainy, when they are deprived by nature of some of the exterior characteristics which I have just assigned to them, or when their long exposure to air has made them lose some of them. Almost all of the masses of flint are subject to having opaque, whitish pockets, or nodes, where the harder substance does not yield as easily to the hammer blow. Some filled cavities, or small crystals or quartz, or nipples of chalcedony, are encountered also. All of these occurrences which interfere with fracturing cause the rejection as useless of masses so affected.

PHYSICAL CHARACTERISTICS

Specific gravity. Blond fire flint from the banks of the Cher has a specific gravity of 26041 [2.60], the water being estimated as 10000 [1.00]. Blackish fire flint from the chalk hills of Rocheguyon is 25954 [2.59].

Note. In this regard fire flint does not differ essentially from all other varieties of flint, the specific gravities of which fall ordinarily between the limits of 26100 [2.61] and 25900 [2.59].

Hardness. The hardness of fire flint is a little greater than that of jasper, but less than that of agate and chalcedony. It is nearly the same as other common flints, *silex vulgaris.*

Fragility. Fire flint is more fragile than most of the other siliceous stones. The blond colored nodule is more fragile than that of brownish color. The latter sparks a little more strongly and causes the battery [frizzen] of the lock to deteriorate a little more quickly.

Proof by collision. Two pieces of fire flint struck vigorously against each other develop more phosphorescence and a stronger odor than any other variety of flint. This odor is consequently characterized by the name of gun flint, by which it is customary to designate it.

CHEMICAL CHARACTERISTICS

Action of air. Fire flint, stripped of its natural crust and exposed for a long time to the weather, appears to take on a second white and friable coating which is nothing more than flint reduced to powder. Its interior loses its greasy look, its translucency, and becomes whitish. In this case, the specific gravity of that which was 25954 [2.59] goes only to 25754 [2.57]. It has lost 2,00 [.02] of the specific gravity it had upon leaving the quarry.

Note. Fire flint is often exceedingly wet when leaving the quarry. It is then dried. If it is exposed too long to air and wind it loses a certain amount of the wetness that was visible at the time it was quarried and can no longer be made into gun flints because it fractures irregularly. The workers take care to reject all that which has lost this favorable degree of dampness. It may be possible to reclaim them by storing them in a cool place, or by covering them with earth. At least by this means they can be saved for work in winter.

Thrown in fragments on a hot iron plate, fire flint jumps and crackles and becomes opaque.

Thrown as a powder on some molten niter, fire flint gives off some sparks, a little flame, and some detonations.

Burned in a dish, fire flint loses, 2,50 [.025] of its specific gravity. It gains in volume, becomes extraordinarily white, and is then very fragmentary and nearly friable. In this state it has the appearance of a beautiful piece of porcelain.

Distilled in a retort and thrust into a very hot fire, fire flint yields a little carbonic acid gas and a quantity of water which accounts for 2,00 [.02] of its specific gravity. There is no indication of the combustible matter which caused the niter to detonate in the preceding experiment.

Note. This water, which seems to be essential to all flints and which I shall name *their radical water,* is the cause of their translucency. Exposure to air in drying them renders them opaque as we have already said. Fire flints are, therefore, among the imperfectly hydrophanous stones, for they only reabsorb with difficulty the water that is necessary to their translucency. This water also contributes to the relationship of their integrating molecules and their brittleness becomes more unequal and greater when it is lost.

This capacity to hold water is such in certain flints that it is possible to make the water leave some of them by pressure alone. On a mineralogical field trip that we made recently to Saint Ouen, Citizens Lievre, Vauquelin and I observed that the blows of a hammer on some masses of flint newly removed from the earth made some of the water leave in the form of an aqueous vapor. The nodules were so saturated that the flake scars were damp and practically wet.

ANALYSIS OF FIRE FLINT

One hundred parts of quite translucent fire flint of brownish color from the hills of Rocheguyon, mixed with 400 grains of very pure

166

potash, were melted together in a silver crucible. After cooling, the mass was washed in water and then supersaturated with muriatic acid. The very clear solution was evaporated to a dry state and then redissolved in water. The silica, separated from this solution by remaining on the filter, was thoroughly washed, dried, and heated until red. It weighed 97 grains. Ammonia was then added to the perfectly clear liquid and a light precipitate, yellowish white in color, was formed. After a thorough washing and drying the precipitate weighed 1 grain. It turned out to be a mixture of alumina and oxide of iron. Carbonate of potash was added to the liquid separated from this small amount of iron and alumina and no precipitate was formed. The wash water was evaporated to dryness and yielded nothing.

The result of the analysis is then:

Silica	97
Alumina and oxide of iron	1
Loss	2
	100

Note. It is remarkable that fire flint should contain only silica and water. The alumina and iron are there in amounts too small to be regarded as essential to its composition or to influence its nature. Quartz also appears, after the analysis that had been made of it, to contain only silica. On the other hand, the more I examine the two substances in nature the more I see them differ one from the other in their behavior. For certainly it cannot be believed that they are identical when it is noted that quartz crystallizes with very great ease, while under the same circumstances flint fails to take on any regular form in the same cavities. The first seeks always to be pure and becomes as clear as water. The second always maintains this cloudy, greasy, translucency which characterizes it. The one is not susceptible to the admission of water into either its structure or its composition. The other remains saturated up to the times of its decomposition. Would the particular characteristics of flints be related solely to this very small quantity of combustible substance, which may be called *oily substance,* which was indicated by the little detonations with niter and which does not appear at all in the distillation? Or did it happen in the stony crystals as noted in the crystals of alum by Citizen Vanquelin who stated, '. . . that the tendency to crystallize in this salt is trebled upon the addition of potash'? Would the simpler flints refuse to crystallize and to form a sort of magma? Would quartz be a more composite stone? Ought there to be some particular combination of the faculty of crystallization and the properties that distinguish it from flint? Only a very exact analysis of thoroughly transparent, crystalline quartz can give us the answer.

I note that Wiegleb gives an analysis of flint called *Feuerstein* very different from ours. This is what he found:

Silica	80
Alumina	18
Lime	2
	100

In the latter case much alumina must have been accidentally included in the flint, for our analysis below, made by Citizen Vauquelin, has all of the exactness that a trained chemist puts into his work. On the other hand, we have seen by other analyses we have made that flint may often include some foreign substances in its composition.

The analysis of the whitish parts that form pockets in the nodules of fire flint gave us:

Silica	98
Oxide of iron	1
Carbonate of lime	2
	101

The analysis of the absolutely opaque part of these same nodules produced.

Silica	97
Oxide of iron	1
Carbonate of lime	5
	103

Finally, the analysis of the white coating that naturally covers the nodules of fire flint gave:

	For 81 grains	For 100 grains	
Silica	70	86,42.	[86.42]
Oxide of iron	1	1,23.	[1.23]
Carbonate of Lime	8	9,88.	[9.88]
Loss	2	2,47.	[2.46]

These subsequent analyses, which have not furnished one atom of alumina, prove that this substance is not essential to the flint, as the absence of lime in the first shows that lime is a foreign host in the latter stones.

LOCATIONS OF DEPOSITS OF FIRE FLINT

In France the principal locations of this stone are in the vicinity of Saint Aignan in the department of Loir-et-Cher and in the department of Indre which occupy the valleys of the Seine and Marne rivers (Map 30 of Cassini).

It is deposited there in calcareous formations such as some of the more or less compact and fine-grained chalks and some of the marls. It occurs in horizontal beds in the form of large and small nodules placed one beside the other. There is no continuity between the masses of chalk above and below when the blocks of flint touch each other.

In twenty beds of flint that are found superimposed one upon the other for a distance of twenty feet, or less, there will be often only one, rarely two, that will yield some good fire flints. In the latter nearly all of the nodules have some *couenne* and in the other beds almost none will have any. The good beds are often followed by means of tunnels to the exclusion of all the others, often a very costly procedure.

On the banks of the Cher, fire flints are exploited by digging pits which reach to the depth of 45 to 50 feet in the soil of the plain. From the pits horizontal galleries are driven into the only good bed that is known there.

On the banks of the Seine, in the hills of Rocheguyon where the chalks are in the form of cliffs, the beds of flint are visible. One of these beds which contains good nodules for gun flints is not more than six fathoms from the upper surface of the great mass of chalk.

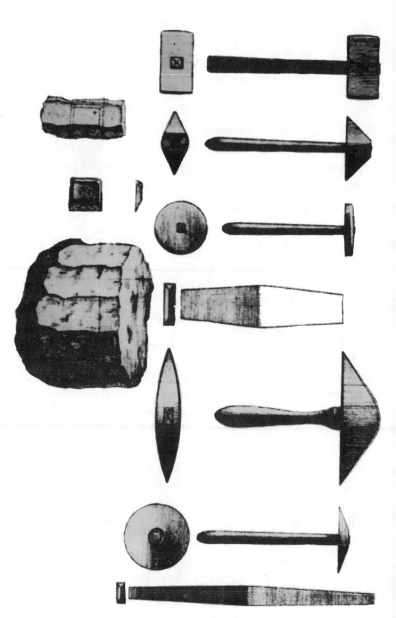

Figure 65. Part of original plate accompanying the papers by Dolomieu and Gillet-Laumont

See Figure 67 for remainder of plate. First four tools described by Dolomieu; Figs. 8-10 are tools described by Salivet in the paper by Gillet-Laumont; Figs. 5-7 represent the nodule, flake, and gun flint respectively.

I have thought these details to be necessary in ascertaining the variety of flint best for gun flints. We return now to the art of making them.

IMPLEMENTS

The tools which serve the worker in fashioning gun flints are four in number.

1. A small iron mace or sledge hammer, with a squared head [Fig. 65]. The weight of it does not exceed two pounds (about 1 kilogram), but may be half of that. The handle is 7 or 8 inches long (19 or 20 cm.) No steel is used in this implement because too much hardness makes the blows too harsh and would shatter the nodule when it is used to break it.

2. A bi-pointed hammer [Fig. 65]. The positions of the points serve to concentrate the strength of the blows. This hammer, ought to be of good, well-tempered steel. It has a weight of not over 16 ounces (5 hectograms) or less than 10 ounces (about 3 hectograms). It is mounted on a handle 7 inches (19 cm.) in length and attached at the center of gravity so that the points are in the appropriate relationships to the hand of the worker. The form and the size of the hammers of different workers vary a little but this arrangement is common to all. It is upon this that the precision of the blow depends.

3. A small tool called a roulette [Fig. 65]. This is in the form of a flat disk, or a segment of a cylinder, 2 in. 4 lines (2⅓ in. or 63 cm.) in diameter and 4 lines (⅓ in.-9mm.) in thickness. Its weight is not more than 12 ounces (about 36 hectograms). It is made of untempered steel and is fastened to a small handle 6 inches (16 cm.) in length by means of a square hole in the center of the disk.

To these four tools a file may be added to sharpen the cutter from time to time.

PROCEDURES

Having chosen a good nodule of fire flint the entire procedure may be divided into four operations:

I. Breaking the block. The worker, seated on the ground, places the nodule on his left thigh and hits downward in little blows with the mace

171

[sledge hammer] to divide it into pieces based more or less on its size. These pieces ought to be one and a half pounds (15 hectograms) in weight, with broad surfaces on which the facets are nearly flat. He is careful not to shatter or shock the nodule by blows that are too sharp or too strong.

II. Cleaving the block, or flaking it. The principal operation in this art is that of flaking the nodule, that is, lifting off flakes of the length, size, and form suitable for making gun flints. It is this operation that requires the greatest craftsmanship and the surest hand.

The stone has no particular cleavage and flakes the same in all directions. The worker holds the piece of the nodule in his left hand, unassisted. He hits with the bi-pointed hammer at the edge of one of the wide faces, produced by the first operation, in order to remove the white crust from the stone in the form of small flakes to expose the flint [Fig. 65]. Next, he continues to remove other flakes where the flint is pure.

These flakes have a width of one and a half inches. (4 cm.), a length of two and a half inches (8 cm.) and a central thickness of two lines (4 to 5 mm.) They are slightly convex on the bottom and, as a result, they leave a slightly concave area in the place they occupied. The flake is bordered longitudinally by two slightly projecting and almost straight lines [Fig. 65]. These kinds of ridges, produced by the rupture of the first flakes, ought to follow the centers of the flakes removed subsequently. Only flakes with these ridges are serviceable in making gun flints.

The flaking of the stone is continued on different sides until natural defects in the nodule render further cleavage impossible, or until it is reduced to a volume too small to receive the blows that force the flint to break.

III. Making the gun flint.

Five parts are distinguished in a gun flint:

1. The bevel [meche], the part that ends in a sloping facet near the edge. It is the sharp edge of the bevel that hits the battery [frizzen] of the gunlock. The bevel ought to be 2 or 3 lines [1/16 to 1/4 of an inch] (5 to 7 mm.) wide. If very wide it would be too fragile; if short it would give fewer sparks.

2. The sides [flancs], which are always a little irregular.

3. The back [talon], which is the part opposed to the bevel and which has the full thickness of the flint.

4. The face [*dessous*] of the flint, which is uniform and a little convex.

5. The bed [*assis*], which is the small face between the bevel and the back. It is slightly concave. The jaws of the cock [hammer] bear upon it and hold the flint in place in the gunlock.

To make gun flints some flakes with at least one longitudinal ridge are chosen. On each one the side which ought to form the bevel, or striking edge is determined. Then the two areas of the flint that are to be the sides and the one that is to be the back are rested, in turn, on the cutter with the convex side down. It is held in place with the left hand and is hit with the roulette. The flint breaks exactly in line with the edge of the cutter as though it had been cut with a knife. Thus the gun flint is fashioned on its sides and back.

IV. The flint, thus reduced to the form it ought to have, is returned to the cutter for the final operation of improving the cutting edge [The operation is called *raffiler*-Trans.] The edge is brought to perfection by resting it against the cutter and hitting it with the roulette five or six times. [The author does not explain that, in addition, the sides are trimmed and the back is rounded through the removal of secondary chips. The finished flint is illustrated in Figure 65].

The entire operation of making a gun flint does not take a minute. A good worker can prepare 1000 good flakes in one day if he has good nodules. In one day he can make 500 gun flints. Thus, in 3 days, he alone will flake and finish 1000 gun flints.

The work leaves much waste. It amounts to about three-quarters because hardly half of the flakes are good, nearly half of the mass of the best nodules cannot be flaked, and it is rare if more than fifty gun flints are furnished by one block.

The flakes which have some crust on them, or which are too thick to use for gun flints, serve to make strike-a-lights. The ones sold in Paris come from the banks of the Seine and are ordinarily brown.

When the gun flints are finished they are sorted into different grades which have different prices based upon the degree of perfection. They sell for from 4 to 6 *decimes* per hundred. There are fine flints and common flints. They are divided into pistol flints, musket flints, and fowling piece flints.

The manufacture of and the trade in gun flints is almost entirely limited to but three communes in the department of Loir-et-Cher and to one in the department of Indre, as I have already said. The localities in Loir-et Cher are the commune of Noyers, 2400 meters to the east northeast of Saint Aignan, that of Couffy, 5600 meters, and that of Meunes, a myriameter [10 kilometers] to the east southwest [*Sic*]. The locality in Indre is the commune of Lye, 9 kilometers to the southeast of Saint Aignan.

Almost 800 of the inhabitants of these communes are engaged in this work. Doubtlessly they have been occupied with it since the time when a piece of flint was substituted for a piece of pyrite, which replaced the match used when muskets were first invented. The workers have excavated almost all of the flint-bearing plain where they live.

One lone worker named Etienne Buffet, having fled from the commune of Meunes [modern Meusnes] and living on the banks of the Siene for more than 30 years, brought his trade there without having trained an apprentice. It is from him that I received the lessons in gun flint making.

There are some small centers in some other parts of France where gun flints are made. One among them is the commune of Maysse on the right bank of the Rhone, 1500 fathoms north northeast of Rochemaure, cantonal seat of the department of Ardeche. None of them has the importance of those near Saint Aignan which export much to foreign parts.

In foreign countries through which I have traveled I know of no place where this art is practiced unless it is in the territory of Vicence [in Italy] and in one canton of Sicily. It is possible that it is practiced in several other places where it is not regarded as important enough to be brought to the attention of the traveler.*

*Norway has neither chalk, nor flint, nor chalcedony, nor agate. See the reports of the Acdemy of Copenhagen, vol. 2 pp. 126, 329. 'Dette land ikke eyer den rett flintesteen.' Sweden has some only in the plains of Scania where Linne found some of it. See his 'Skanska Resa . . .'Denmark has some chalk hills containing flint on the island of Sjaelland at the bailiwicks of Vordingborg and Taxoe. The most notable is that called 'Stevnsklint'. Hacquet has recognized some good fire flints in Podolia and Pocutia in some hills of chalk and marl on the banks of Podhorce at its junction with the Dniester River [Translator's note: This area seems to be in the western part of the Ukrainian S.S.R.] The imperial [Russian] army, following the findings of Hacquet, are supplied now with gun flints in this part of old Poland. The same naturalist has given a detailed description of the fabrication of gun flint with a figure showing the tools used there in Volume 5 of the MAGAZIN HELVETIQUE. He states that the flints of Podolia are superior for this use to those of France as well as England. The storehouse of this flint was at Nizniow in 1789. More than 90,000 of then were prepared there in two months.

Coquebert.

EXTRAIT

D'un Mémoire du citoyen Salivet, *sur la fabrication des pierres à fusil dans les départemens de l'Indre et de Loir-et-Cher ;*

Par F. P. N. GILLET-LAUMONT :

Avec l'indication de quelques autres lieux où il s'en fabrique également.

Depuis la lecture du mémoire du citoyen *Dolomieu* à l'institut, le conseil des mines a eu connaissance d'un mémoire sur la fabrication des pierres à fusil des environs de Saint-Aignan, fait par le citoyen *Salivet* commissaire envoyé en l'an 2 sur les lieux par l'administration des armes portatives. Ce mémoire intéressant, ayant pour but principal la partie administrative, contient plusieurs faits déjà rapportés dans celui du citoyen *Dolomieu*, et d'autres qui ajoutent des détails nouveaux ou des éclaircissemens utiles à cet art intéressant. On va rapporter ici ce qu'il contient de plus important relativement à l'art.

D'après le citoyen *Salivet,* les deux communes où l'on fait le plus de pierres à fusil, sont, sur la rive gauche du Cher, celle de Couffy composée d'une infinité de hameaux où demeurent une grande partie des ouvriers caillouteurs, et celle de Meunes où il y en a un assez grand nombre : les carrières d'où ils extraient les cailloux, occupent un espace de plus d'une lieue carrée (seize kilomètres carrés). Dans la commune de Lye il y a peu d'ouvriers, et dans celle de Noyers, sur la rive droite du Cher, il y en a encore moins.

[marginal note: Communes des environs de St.-Aignan où l'on fait le plus de pierres à fusil.]

Figure 66. Title page of article by Gillet-Laumont.

175

EXTRACT FROM A REPORT BY CITIZEN SALIVET THE MAKING OF GUN FLINTS IN THE DEPARTMENTS OF INDRE AND LOIR-ET-CHER
by F.P.N. Gillet-Laumont.
Translation by Carlyle S. Smith

Since the reading of the report by Citizen Dolomieu, the *Conseil des Mines* has had brought to its attention an account of the manufacture of gun flints in the vicinity of Saint Aignan by Citizen Salivet, a commissioner sent to the localities in the Year 2 [1793-94] by the Small Arms Committee. This interesting report, largely concerned with administrative matters, contains many facts already reported in the account by Citizen Dolomieu and some others which add some new details, or useful clarifications, in regard to this interesting art. The most important data relative to the art will be reported here.

According to Citizen Salivet, the two communes where most of the gun flints are made are on the left bank of the Cher. A large proportion of the flint workers live in Couffy, which is made up of many hamlets, and in Meunes where there is also a fairly large number of them. The quarries where they take out the nodules occupy an area more than one league square (16 kilometers square). In the commune of Lye there are few workers, and in the commune of Noyers, on the right bank of the Cher, there are even fewer.

The soil covering the beds where the nodules are found is generally of mediocre quality. The surface of it is sandy and good for vineyards. The low places are wet and contain some beautiful meadows.

The nodules suitable for the manufacture of gun flints are found in horizontal beds at the depth of fourteen and a half to sixteen meters (about 45 to 50 feet by the old measure) in soft and gellatinous earth that is calcareous and argillaceous. They are covered with a crust of white chalk from one to three centimeters in thickness.

The flint workers are rarely landowners. Five or six of them will go together and buy the right to dig in about one half *arpent* [The *arpent* constitutes between one and one-and-a-half acres.—[Translator]. Around the middle of the Year 2 they were paying from 400 to 500 *Francs*. They work the bed of nodules good for gun flints by means of tunnels at a depth of about 16 meters (nearly 50 feet) to which they descend in several small shafts dug in tiers. They call these *carriers* [quarries], *caves* [hollows], or *crocs* [hooks].

They begin by scooping out a broad excavation that is nearly round in the typically sandy soil. The initial excavation measures from 13 to 16 decimeters (4 to 5 feet) in depth [Fig. 67]. After having penetrated into more solid ground they open a shaft of rectangular form from 16 to 20 decimeters (5 to 6 feet) in length, 7 decimeters (2 feet) in width, and dug to a depth of 30 to 32 decimeters (9 to 10 feet).

Then they make a shaft of similar dimensions but not in plumb with the first. For this they work horizontally for a distance of 6 to 7 decimeters (2 feet) for the entire length of one side of the first shaft, forming a kind of niche. From this they sink the second shaft vertically to the same depth as the first. If necessary, they dig a third and then a fourth shaft in the same fashion as the second in order to reach the bed of nodules suitable for working.

When they have reached it they extend very low horizontal galleries where they work on their knees. The galleries are extended radially, using the shaft as a center, and are dug as far as a light is able to burn, quite often beyond the limits of the area for which they have acquired the right to dig. Finally, they connect the galleries with one another, leaving pillars to support the roof.

They remove the flint nodules with great speed, throwing them from hand to hand up to each of the five or six resting places formed by the bottoms of the shafts arranged in tiers. They take out the earth only from the first galleries. They successively refill the earlier excavations with earth from the later ones.

They work underground only in the morning. Then they divide the flint nodules into portions as equal as possible. They break them up right at the edge of the shaft with the mace, rejecting those which do not have a good color, or which have white inclusions or which contain chalk at the center, as often happens. They remove flakes from the others with the bi-pointed hammer, leaving the *grolles** on the ground with the chips, and carry away the flakes to their thatched cottages. There, aided by their wives and children, they hew them on the cutter with the roulette and make them into a *patet*, a *boucaniere*, a *grande fuye*, a *petite fuye*, pistol flint, etc., etc.

Two varieties of flint appropriate for the making of gun flints are recognized, one blond and the other brown. The blond variety is found in the communes of Meunes, Noyers, and Lye. They are of even

177

color and make fire well with the battery [frizzen]. The brown variety comes from the commune of Couffy, a short league from Meunes. The latter variety is often spotted with white and is regarded as too hard because they damage the battery in a short time.

The workers of Meunes appear to be the most skillful in the making of gun flints, and yet they are not sure of making a flint of a specific form. It is only after the flake falls from the block that they can judge to what use it is appropriate. Ten or twelve different kinds are made, but there are only three or four which are suitable for military arms.

As a result of removing flakes from a nodule some flakes have inclined planes on the right and left sides with very pronounced edges. On these no backs are present and they are reserved for the making of flints with two bevels, or for two blows (a double flint—Translator]. It is so called because after one edge is worn out the other can be used by turning the flint [in the jaws of the cock—Translator]. They are ordinarily a little thin and the edge turned toward the clamp of the cock breaks off and becomes useless. The French armed forces do not use them but they are much sought after by the Dutch and Spanish.

When the nodules come out of the earth they sometimes contain too much moisture which may be seen when flaking them and which collects at the center in droplets. These cannot be worked properly. The flint workers let them dry for a few hours, in the summer in the sun, in the winter by the fire. But those that have been exposed too long to the sun and the open air, like those found on the surface, cannot be worked any more. The merchants who store gun flints are careful to keep them in a cool, closed place.*

The tools reported by Citizen Salivet differ little in form from those described by Citizen Dolomieu.

---

*The thick flakes with crust on them are called "grolles."They do not hold well in the jaws of the cock and are used to make strike-a-lights.

*It would doubtlessly be well for the individual warehouses to halt the excessive desiccation that flints acquire in dry places. It gives them a short scaley cleavage which renders their edges more obtuse and diminishes their ability to detach particles of steel from the battery which, igniting, produce the spark. (Note by Citizen Gillet)

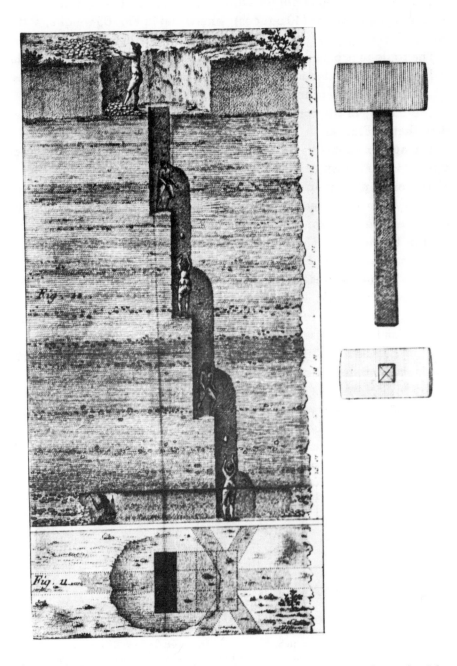

Figure 67. Ground plan and profile of a flint mine as described by
Salivet in the paper by Gillet-Laumont.

The mace is the same as that in Fig. 65.

The bi-pointed hammer is of the same form, but is longer and weighs 25 hectograms (40 ounces), where that in Fig. 65 weighs, at the most, 10 hectograms.

The roulette is broader, made thinner toward the edges, and weighs only 7 ounces (21 decagrams); whereas that in Fig. 65 weighs almost 12 ounces (36 decagrams).

The cutter, in the form of the joiner's iron dog, is much narrower than that in Fig. 65.

The author claims that nodules appropriate for the manufacture of gun flints are known only in France*. He cites the accounts of the merchants of Saint Aignan which prove that they ship considerable quantities of them each year to Holland, Spain, England, etc.** He tells that when the Emperor Joseph II came to France in 1776 he sent some people to Meunes. There, they had great difficulty in choosing a young man to accompany them to Austria. This young man returned to Meunes some months later, saying that he had not found nodules suitable for the work. The attachment that flint workers have for their locale would seem to indicate that they have not found an opportunity to practice their art elsewhere. On the other hand, it appears that some fire flint can be found in the chalks of former Champagne and Picardy and in some other places in France.

The district of Saint Aignan, in the Year 2, tested a nodule coming from Bougival to the west of Paris on the banks of the Seine near the Marly works where the greater part of the strike-a-lights sold in Paris are made. The nodule from Bougival lent itself perfectly to the work and yielded 131 flints appropriate for firearms.

---

*This is not true now, although it might have been in the past. Many countries have begun to use the flint found there in making gun flints. In the work entitled "The Art of the Mines" (in German BERGBAUKUNDE), Volume 2, Article III, one reads that flints are made for the Austrian military service from flint found in beds alternating with chalk on both sides of the Adige in the Italian Tyrol, near Avio. The foothills which contain them are called 'le Felv (SIC) del Monte Baldo.' They prevail at the foot of a mountain of that name in the valley of 'Acque nere.' In the same district many flints are found scattered on the surface of the ground.

Ch. C. (Charles Coquebert)

**In the Year 2 there were thirty million in storage in Saint Aignan and the vicinity.

[THE WORK OF CITIZEN TONNELIER]

Citizen Tonnelier, keeper of the mineralogical collection near the *Conseil des Mines,* was recently in the department of Yonne. When passing through the Cerilly district he was struck by the quantity of fire flint that he saw (Maps 46 and 47 of Cassini). Having arrived in the commune of Cerilly, he observed some flint workers' flakes and occupied himself in collecting all the details about a small gun flint factory which he found there. He reported some of the data to the *Societe Philomatique.* We will extract some particulars from the work of this naturalist which seem appropriate here.

The small commune of Cerilly is situated in a mountainous countryside, the barren soil of which is suitable only for rye and buckwheat (*polygonum fagopyrum*) and where much cider and very little wine is made. The layer of humus is two decimeters thick at the most. Below it is an argillaceous marl which serves to fertilize the land. It is in this marl that one finds the fire flints which the industry of some of the inhabitants converts into gun flints.

The hills that conceal the best flint in the largest quantities form a group bearing the name of Mont Equillon. These nodules also occur on the surface and in the ravines with which the countryside is furrowed. The roads are heaped with them and all of the houses are built of them. The waste stone from the work is not used there because of the distance from the quarries being exploited in this department. Although until the present they have made gun flints only in the commune of Cerilly and in the village of Vallees, which depend upon them, good flint for this use is found over most of the district as well, notably in the communes of Foureaudin, Coulours, and in that of Cerisiers which is the cantonal seat.

This small industry was established about 80 years ago in Cerilly. It is said that the people from the part of France which was then known as Berry, having been called into this canton on some special business, noted a great similarity between the flints that it contained and those that they used to work in their birthplace. [The old province of Berry included the present departments of Cher and Indre—Translator]. They tried to make the same use out of them and succeeded during the six months that they stayed in Cerilly, in making a rather large quantity of gun flints which they sold to some merchants from Troyes.

181

An inhabitant of the commune examined their tools, had copies made of them, and, after their departure, applied himself to the same type of work with success. He taught his children the art that he had seen practiced. This art is still perpetuated exclusively by this family. There are still only three men who work at it, and then only when not busy with the demands of agriculture.

These farmer flintworkers do not extract the flint in a regular manner. They are content with the digging of small holes which have constricted openings and which are enlarged toward the bottom. Usually these excavations do not go deeper than 18 to 20 decimeters. The fire flint is more often found there in little clusters than in regular connected beds. When these clusters are exhausted they open another hole to one side.

The implements that they use in the work differ a little from those which Citizen Dolomieu has described. They are copies of those that the flintworkers from former Berry brought there at the beginning of the century. In this respect it may be interesting to set forth their forms and uses in order to be in position to appraise the changes that have been made in them since.

They consist, first, of an iron sledge hammer, or mace, rounded at the ends, about four centimeters wide and eight centimeters long. It differs little from that described by Citizen Dolomieu [Fig. 65] and serves in the same way to break the silicious blocks into pieces of one to two pounds each.

Secondly, there is a hammer with one point with a body measuring from two to three centimeters in thickness. It is elongated only on one side. One point, rounded and shod with steel, serves in detaching the flakes. The head measures eight centimeters overall and is pierced all the way through to receive the handle. This implement seems to be inferior to those with two points, [Fig. 65], in use around Saint Aignan because the handle is not set at center of gravity. This ought to make it subject to turning in the hand of the worker. Also it has but one point and ought to last only half as long without need of repair.

Thirdly, there is an implement consisting of a steel blade about two decimeters long, six to eight millimeters thick, and two decimeters wide. This blade is pierced in one of its wider faces by a hole that serves in attaching the handle. It is a little rounded at the ends and serves the same function as the roulettes, [Fig. 65], in trimming the flakes. It seems to require more skill in handling and to need repairs more frequently.

Fourthly, there is a cutter in the form of a joiners' dog, resembling that described by Citizen Dolomieu, [Fig. 65]. It serves in the same way to support the flakes in order to cut them with the single bladed tool. This cutter is set in one end of a block of wood across from and at the same level as the seated worker. The block is hollowed out in the middle to receive the gun flints which the worker throws there after they have been cut.

The specific gravity of the fire flint from Cerilly, after having been broken for some time, is 2.5942 [2.59]. Its color is brown. The gun flints made from this material are sold ordinarily by the merchants of Troyes which is but six myriameters [60 kilometers] from Cerilly. At the beginning of the present war this commune supplied 6000 hundred-weight of flints for the use of the armies.

As a result of these reports it is known that centers for the making of gun flints are as follows in the territories of the Republic:

	DEPARTMENTS	CANTONS	COMMUNES	COLORS
Large factory	Loir-et-Cher	Saint Aignan	Meunes	Blond
			Noyers	Blond
			Couffy	Brown
Large factory	Indre	Villentrois	Lye	Blond
Small factory	Ardeche	Rochemaure	Maysse	Brown?
Small factory	Yonne	Cerisiers	Cerilly	Brown
Small factory	Seine-et-Oise	La Rocheguyon	La Rocheguyon	Brown
Experimental	Seine-et-Oise	Marly	Bougival	Brown

THE MANUFACTURE OF GUN FLINTS

This article originally appeared in the "The Saturday Magazine" published by John William Parker, West Strand, London, in 1838. It was printed in two columns with illustrations inserted in various places. In recopying, the form as been kept as originally printed. The illustrations have been enlarged, but the lines and captions have been very closely adhered to. "The Saturday Magazine" was published "in weekly numbers, price one penny, and in monthly parts price six-pence". *SJG*

S. James Gooding, Editor of the Ontario Arms Collectors' Association Bulletin, (now The Canadian Journal of Arms Collecting) discovered this article and reprinted it in their first issue in 1952. It is reprinted here by his permission. It was reprinted for the second time in April of 1957 by "Muzzle Blasts" the magazine of the National Muzzle Loading Rifle Association. *TMH*

The art of making gun flints was formerly kept a profound secret, at least in France and Germany. The kind of stone employed, is that species of silex, or flint, which is found in irregularly shaped lumps in the chalk formations of the earth.

The masses of flint which are best fitted for the purpose, consist of those of a convex surface, approaching to globular, the knobbed and branched flints being generally full of imperfections. The best flint nodules are in general from two to twenty pounds in weight; they should be unctuous, or rather shining internally, with a grain so fine as to be imperceptible to the eye. The colour should be uniform in the same nodule, and may vary from honey-yellow to a blackish-brown; it is necessary that the fracture should be smooth and equal, and somewhat conchoidal, hollowed like a shell, and should be partially transparent at the thin edges.

Four tools are necessary in the manufacture of flints. 1. An iron hammer, Fig. 1, with a square head, not more than two pounds in weight, and seven or eight inches in length: 2. a hammer of well-hardened steel, Fig. 2, with two points, a handle seven inches long, and from ten to sixteen ounces in weight: 3. a disk hammer, or roller, Fig. 3, like a solid wheel or cylinder, two inches and one-third in diameter, and not exceeding twelve ounces in weight; it is made of steel not hardened, and has a handle six inches long. 4. a chisel, Fig. 4, tapering and bevelled at both ends, which should be made of steel not hardened, six, seven, or eight inches long, and two inches wide, [Fig.68]. With these tools the flints are formed in the following manner:—

The workman, seated on the ground, places the nodule of flint on his left thigh, and applies slight strokes with the square hammer to divide it into smaller pieces of about a pound and half in weight, with broad surfaces and an almost even fracture. He then holds the piece of flint in his left hand, not supported, and strikes with the pointed hammer on the edges of the great planes produced by the first breaking by which means the white coating of the flint is removed in the form of small scales, and the mass of flint itself laid bare, as shown in Fig. 5; after this he continues to chip off similar scaly portions from the pure mass of flints as A A A, Fig. 6, which is a cross section or plan of Fig. 5, the shaded portions showing the points removed at each blow, [Fig. 68]. These portions are nearly an inch and a half wide, two and a half inches long, and their thickness in the middle is about one-sixth of an inch; they are slightly convex below, and consequently leave in the part of the flint from which they are separated, a space slightly concave, longitudinally bordered by two rather projecting straight lines or ridges. These ridges produced by the separation of the two scales, must naturally constitute nearly the middle of the subsequent piece;

and such scales alone as have their ridges thus placed in the middle are fit for gun flints. In this manner the workman continues to split or chip the mass of flint in various directions, until the defects usually found in the interior render it impossible to make the fracture required, or until the piece is reduced too much to be easily broken.

To shape the gun flint out of these scales, he selects such only as possess the requisite form; to ascertain this, it is necessary to understand the parts to be distinguished in a gun flint. These are five in number; A the sloping facet, B the sides, C the back, D the under surface, which should be rather convex, and E the upper facet, between the tapering edge and the back, [Fig. 68].

In order to fashion the flint, those scales are selected which contain at least one of the ridges F or A; he fixes on any tapering border of the scale to form the striking edge; he then divides the scale into pieces, of the proper width of the flint, by means of his chisel; this tool is driven into a solid block of wood, with one of its edges upwards; that part of the flint is placed across this edge where the separation is intended to take place, and a blow from the roulette, or round hammer, on the upper surface divides it as cleanly as if it were cut; the back of the flint is then made square by the same means.

The last operation is to trim or give the flint a smooth and equal edge; this is done by turning the stone and placing the edge of its taper on the chisel, and striking it a few blows with the round hammer.

Figure 68. Illustrations of the tools used in the manufacture of English gun flints, and the procedure followed in striking off flakes from the flint nodule.

(As shown in the article which originally appeared in the SATURDAY MAGAZINE in 1838.)

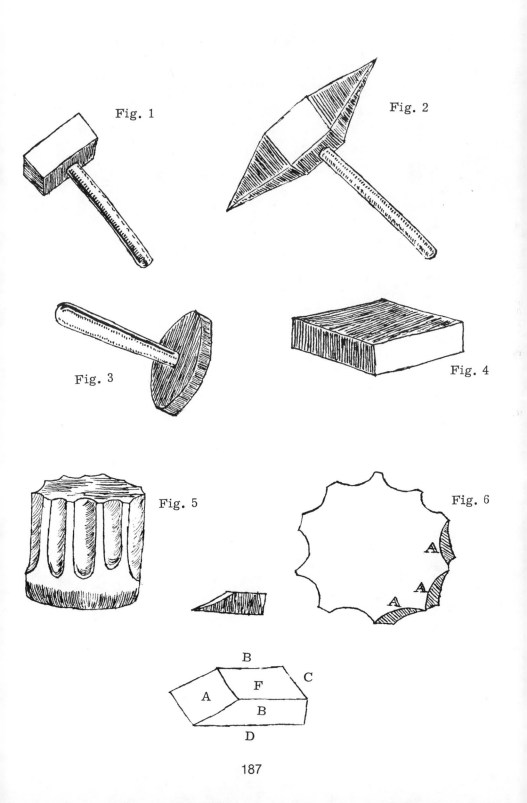

Fig. 1

Fig. 2

Fig. 3

Fig. 4

Fig. 5

Fig. 6

B

C

A F

B

D

187

[Chapter 13]
CONCLUDING COMMENTS ON GUNFLINTS
T.M. Hamilton

The literature on gun flints is limited. The paper by Arthur Wood-
ward (1951), referred to by Carlyle Smith in his Introduction to the two
French reports, has been reprinted because of its special importance.
That article includes among its references almost all of the pertinent
material published to date with the possible exception of *THE
MANUFACTURE OF GUNFLINTS,* which originally appeared in the
SATURDAY MAGAZINE in 1838, and which is also reprinted.

Dr. Smith's Introduction in the Dolomieu and the Gillet-Laumont
reports is as welcome an addition to the literature on gun flints as his
translations, which finally make these important sources available to
the English speaking student. Between them they contain answers to
some rather perplexing questions. It might be well, therefore, to present some additional information so the reader can better appreciate
the significance of the preceeding papers.

One of the most common artifacts of the contact periods is the gun
flint. In Missouri, gun flints have been found on sites which have not
yet produced a single other gun part. It is true that we find ample
evidence of trade, such as copper kettles, iron axes, and iron knives,
but, aside from the presence of gun flints, we have no reason to say
that these people had firearms. We find that gun flints are occasionally
the one and only item (1) indicating the presence of guns, and (2) furnishing a possible clue to (a) the probable source of supply or (b) the
approximate date when the trade was being carried on.

The possibilities of interpretation inherent in the ubiquitous gun
flint deserves particular attention, for in that single item lies a potentially valuable and exact dating tool.

Another pioneer in the study of gun flints was John Witthoft, Curator of the Pennsylvania State Museum in 1960. According to Mr. Witthoft, before 1700 the Indians made most of the gun flints found in Pennsylvania, New York and the surrounding area. From his description these 17th Century native flints of the East are indistinquishable from those made by the Osage in Missouri 100 years later.[1] The Osage flints are of mottled chert and of almost any color or combination of colors, as with projectile points. They tend to be square and, invariably, all four edges are carefully worked to an edge by secondary chipping.

In contrast with the native flints of sometimes excellent workmanship, Witthoft found that the early 17th Century European flints are "crudely spalled to shape". They are made from poor quality chalk flints, probably taken from outcroppings in Denmark or Jutland. He sent samples to Europe in an attempt to get them identified, but with little success. He concluded that the flint from which they were made was probably float and not quarried.[2]

The French flint first made its appearance in small quantities about 1675. These were "wedge-shaped spalls, not lenticular". This gun flint was the prevailing type from about 1700 to 1750. The gun flints used during the French and Indian Wars are found to be approximately 50 percent these wedge shaped spalls and 50 percent the more convential form such as found in Missouri.

English flints do not make their appearance until about 1750, and they are of the usual prism-like form. By 1775 all gun flints are prism-shaped. The astonishing fact is that over 95 percent of gun flints found in camps occupied during the American Revolution, including even the British, are of French origin!

During the War of 1812, half of the flints used were French and half British.

Witthoft found the following distribution of 75 gun flints from a Wyandot Indian town of 1748, which was near West Pittsburgh, Pennsylvania:

French flint	60%	(Of different color and texure than those mined later.)
British flint	10%	
Other	30%	(Probably French float flint.)
	100%	
Prism-form	10%	
Wedge-shaped	90%	
	100%	

Mr. Witthoft concludes his comments with the observation that, "Our information on the history of gun flints is still imperfect, but it is possible to do some fairly precise dating on the basis of small samples through the combined data of typology and lithic materials."[3]

Ignoring for the moment Witthoft's comment about the earlier types of gun flints and confining our attention to those of conventional manufacture, we see the following picture emerging:

The technique of striking off long prismatic blades preparatory to making the individual flints appears to have been developed about 1750. Witthoft has observed that from about 1750 to 1800 the vast majority were of French manufacture. This is true even in the British camps of the Revolutionary period! As difficult as this fact has been to accept in the past, it is no longer so for, by now referring to the French reports in this volume, we find Salivet stating that the merchants of Saint Aignan "ship considerable quantities" of gun flints each year to Holland, Spain, England, etc. In a footnote Coquebert comments that in 1793 there were thirty million gun flints in storage in that vicinity! It follows then that the phrase "considerable quantities" was a rather modest description of the export trade in French gun flints and that not only the English army used them in vast quantities, but that the English and Colonial traders were passing them along to their Indian customers. Consequently, for this period at least, and unless modified by other considerations, the mere presence of French gun flints on a site does not mean that the guns in which they were used were also of French manufacture, nor that the trade itself was basically French.

The Osage sites in Missouri deal with time periods which are approximately 20 years later than those observed by Witthoft, and prove that the French gun flints still predominated. It is true that the balance was not so unfavorable to the English as it was in the Eastern part of the United States, but the English flints were still in the minority. In fact, whenever it is found that the English flints out-number the French —even though the total quantity involved is only eight or ten—the situation is so unusual that it calls for a recount and additional speculation.

On the other hand, up the Missouri River there appears to be a tendency for the majority of the flints to be English, rather than French. The following table shows the comparison of French, English, and Native flints found in the collections in one institution. It is possible that the flints under Collection "D" and "Misc" should not be included in a tabulation primarily concerned with village sites, but if they were eliminated, the predominance of English flints would be even greater—71 to 45 in place of 80 to 62. The two last groups were included in an attempt to approximate the true situation in the Nebraska area as a whole.

SITE	FRENCH	ENGLISH	NATIVE
Bu 1	4	2	1
Hw 1			1
N 5			1
Pk 1	1	28	
Wn 9	40	34	4
Wt 1		3	
Wt 6		4	
Collection "D"	1	4	1
Misc.	16	5	
Total	62	80	8

Distribution of gun flints by village sites found in the collections of the Nebraska State Historical Society Museum, Lincoln, Nebraska.

This distinct shift from a predominance of French flints in the eastern United States, representing the period from about 1750 to 1800, to a condition of slight predominance in Missouri, from about 1770 to 1820, to a position of English flint predominance on the upper Missouri, where the trade flourished from about 1810 to 1870, seems to be distinctly significant. Actually, the relative percentages directly reflect the gradual emergence of England as, not only a world trader, but also a manufacturer of trade goods. It follows that where more French flints than English are found, the probabilities are that the historical period lay in the last half of the 18th Century, and the definite English predominance indicates an historical period after 1800.

Another interesting sidelight is revealed in the relative percentages of native flints to those of European manufacture. Witthoft found that during the early period of contact, that is before 1700 and while the Indian still retained his pre-contact skill in making projectile points, he made most of his own gun flints. This is only natural since making one of those objects is relatively easy when compared with making the traditional projectile point.

It seems that the Osage in Missouri retained their flint flaking skills to a surprisingly late date for beautifully chipped gun flints coming from sites dating no earlier than the last quarter of the 18th Century have been found.

On the other hand, native gun flints on the upper Missouri appear to be a rarity. A total of only eight in the entire collection of the Nebraska State Historical Society Museum could be found—and one of these is questionable. It may well be the base of a straight stemmed projectile point. It is known that the Plains Indians were using metal arrow heads long before the white traders themselves reached the area. They were getting them by trade with the intervening tribes, so the art of working

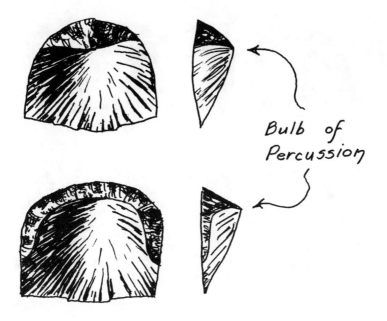

Bulb of Percussion

Figure 69A. Spall Gun flints.

An early form of the gun flint which makes its first appearance in about 1675 and was almost completely supplanted by the conventional prismatic form by 1775. These spalls appear to have been struck individually from small boulders of flint, well rounded by water or glacial action. The upper gun flint is from Fort Frederica, 1736-1748, while the lower was found among the collections of the Nebraska State Historical Society Museum, Lincoln. Both of these gun flints were made from a fine grained grey chert and are presumed to be of French origin.

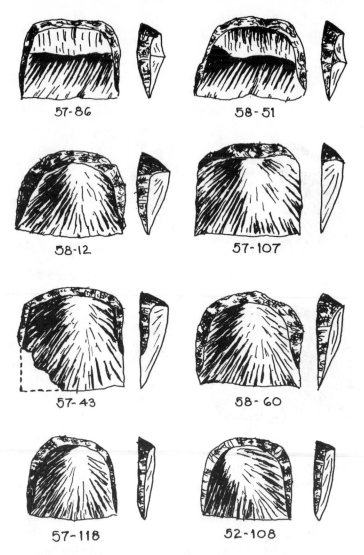

Figure 69B. Gun flints and Spall Gun flints from Fort Frederica.
Loaned for study by W.H. Glover, Superintendent, No's. 57-86 and 58-51 are typical
French flints. As explained in the text, gun flints of French manufacture predominate
even on purely English sites, such as this, during the 18th Century. The remaining are
spall gun flints, presumably also of French manufacture. Dimensions of flints: No.
57-86, 1 1/2 in. x 1 1/4 in.; 58-51, 1 7/16 in. x 1 1/8 in.; 59-12, 1 5/8 in. x 1 3/8 in.;
57-107, 1 3/8 in. x 1 5/16 in.; 57-43, 1 7/16 in. x 1 7/16 in.; 58-60, 1 3/16 in. x 1 1/8 in.;
57-118, 1 in. x 1 in.; 52-108, 1 in. x 15/16 in.

flint in most areas had undoubtedly declined considerably by the time the first guns became available.

There still remains for discussion one of the most interesting facets of the gun flint problem. Witthoft speaks in his letter of an early French form introduced in about 1675, which was the prevailing type from about 1700 to 1750. He describes it as a "wedge shaped spall, not lenticular".[4]

From a small collection of four gun flints picked up on the parade ground of Fort Frederica, which is now a National Monument near Brunswick, Georgia, and which was occupied by the English from 1736 to 1748, three of them are instantly recognized as "wedged shaped spalls".

These gun flints are nothing more than individual spalls knocked off the surfaces of rounded boulders of chert. Examination of the original surface still remaining on the spall, indicates that the parent boulders were quite small, possibly the size of a man's fist and that they had been rounded by stream action or possibly glacial action. Reconstruction of their manufacture from, admittedly, no other evidence than the spalls themselves, they were knocked off the boulders individually, and then trimmed down to size. All the spalls observed bear some resemblance to the conventional French flint inasmuch as they all have the rounded or "gnawed" heel which characterizes it.

Since attention was focused upon these wedge shaped spalls a few of them have been found in Missouri and one in the collections of the Nebraska State Historical Society Museum at Lincoln. Figure 69A includes a drawing of the Nebraska flint which bears their catalogue number 472 and was found in Webster County. It is made from a fine grained grey chert.

Smith, in his introduction to the French gun flint articles, speaks of five black flints in a sample purchased from Bannerman which were also made from spalls, and later in the same paragraph he states that "grey flints of this form have been picked up on the surface in South Dakota" while "two occurred in the collections of the Kansas Monument site." Smith's assumption that the spalls from black flint were an incidental by-product in the manufacture of regular gun flints is very likely correct. This conviction received further support from John Wittoft. The following is his notation:

"The collections of the University Museum, Philadelphia, Pa., include a large collection of flints, in-process material, and flint-maker's tools collected from the shops at Brandon, England by Henry Mercer about 1892. There is one sample of wedge-shaped flints among the varieties represented by samples labeled with their trade-names. These are mainly large tinder-box flints, and were broken from the nuclei after the flint-knapper had removed all of the blades that could be struck from the core. Thus the primitive free-flaking technique survived almost into our time as a subsidiary process, adapting to use core-remnants from which conventional flints could not be struck."

On the other hand, this does not allow us to make the same assumption for spall gun flints made from chert. Since European gun flints are always made from a translucent flint of relatively high quality, it is obvious that a gun spall of chert is either of Native manufacture or made by an entirely different European technique. Since the style of manufacture is definitely not in the Native tradition, and since they are known to be found on the parade ground at Fort Frederica, the most plausible explanation is that they are of early 17th Century European manufacture, and that they support Witthoft's original estimate of their date of manufacture.

The presence of spall gun flints in North Dakota does not violate the established history of white penetration since la Verendrye was in that area in about 1740. On the other hand, the appearance of this same type of gun flint in the collections of the Kansas Monument site is more difficult to explain since its occupational dates of 1775—1800[5] seem to be a little late for gun spalls.

In closing it should be pointed out that the Nebraska State Historical Society Museum has a remarkable collection of 86 French gun flints found in a cache in 1907 in Genoa County. These are musket flints approximately 1 inch in width and from 1 1/2 to 1 7/8 inches in length, and are in new condition. The card states that the donor is unknown. It is unfortunate indeed that circumstances surrounding the finding of this cache can no longer be determined, but they were probably buried by some adventurer in that area during the closing years of the 18th Century.

1. Witthoft, John (1958) Personal Letter.
2. ibid.
3. ibid.
4. ibid.
5. Smith, Carlyle P. (1960) Personal Letter.

III

DATING
AND
IDENTIFICATION

[Chapter 14]
How To Determine Dates And Origin
by
T.M. Hamilton

If the recovery of gun parts is to have any meaning, two questions must be answered: (1) what was the approximate date of manufacture, and (2) where was it made? Of the two questions, the determination of the probable date of manufacture is by far the more simple; especially when the part in question is the firing mechanism. To decide just where the part was made—whether it is of French, English, Spanish, German, Swedish or Belgian origin—is a much more complex problem. This does not mean that the determination of origin of gun parts is an impossibility, or even a questionable procedure. The present difficulty is that the study has not yet progressed far enough to have accumulated the necessary background of information.

Identification of a gun part depends upon the orderly recognition of certain characteristics, which are usually secondary features to an advanced gun collector. Those features which are of primary interest to the gun collector are proofmarks, names, decorative designs, and sometimes even the actual date when the gun or lock was made. Needless to say such details are seldom found on gun parts which have been underground for 150, 200, or possibly 300 years.

A gun is in excellent condition if it has not yet completely lost its wooden stock through decay; but usually we are dealing with a gun part or fragment badly pocked with rust. Consequently, to determine the exact model of the gun from which it came is a refinement beyond the possibilities available. If an estimated date of manufacture to within a plus or minus period of ten years, can be made, it is considered a major step. As for determining the model, that may be done if it is a well established military weapon, or if the gun was made in the last half of the 19th Century. Otherwise, it is a probability that the gun from which the part came was not of any particular "model," as that term is used today, but a "type."

These "types" were made in various small gunshops scattered over Europe and, later, in America, and the gradations in variations were endless; the variations depending more upon the whims of the individual makers than upon anything else. It was not until the opening years of the last century, when the smoothbore finally became standardized as the Northwest Gun, that the firearms traded to the Indian achieved any marked degree of uniformity.

The ignition system, or gun lock, is the one part which is the most easily recognized by the nonspecialist. However, there are many other gun parts which can be used for purposes of identification. The buttplates are of particular promise. Triggers, trigger plates, or isolated frizzens, have not been utilized but that does not necessarily mean that they are without diagnostic value. As information is accumulated they may prove to be quite useful. Surprisingly enough, gun barrel fragments, have proven to be one of the most profitable items for study.

There were six ignition systems for firearms developed and used before the introduction of the metallic cartridge, and before the repeating gun became standard equipment toward the close of the last century.

The matchlock, used from approximately 1425 to 1675.

The wheellock, used from approximately 1525 to 1600.

The snaphaunce, used from approximately 1600 to 1700.

The miquelet, used from approximately 1600 to 1825.

The flintlock, used from approximately 1625 to 1825.

The caplock, used from approximately 1825 to 1875.

The above dates are not to be taken too literally. In the first place, no one can say definitely just when a given ignition system was first introduced into a frontier area nor when it was last used; and, in the second place, the dates have been rounded off to the nearest quarter century for convenience.

During the period covered by the American Fur Trade, the flintlock was the most important ignition system used. Therefore, we will confine ourselves, with but few exceptions, to that one type. Archaeologists working in Florida or the Southwest may find examples of the miquelet, an ignition system consistently favored by the Spaniards; and early 17th Century sites on the east coast will produce examples of the matchlock, wheellock, and snaphaunce.

Since the flintlock, next to the clock, was the most complex mechanism in the hands of the average man until well into the 19th

Century, its diagnostic possibilities seem to be tremendous. For instance, if only the lockplate is present, having been stripped of all its lock parts, more information can be gained from a careful inspection than merely its outline. If the flashpan is gone, obviously it was removable. Not all locks had that feature. If the inside of the plate shows a countersunk frizzen spring screw hole, it is positive evidence that the screw was inserted from the inner side of the plate and threaded into a hole in the frizzen spring. That is known as a "hidden frizzen spring screw" and considered by some to be a French characteristic.

It must be emphasized, however, that determination of origin is not quite so simple. Certainly, no single detail can be regarded as proof that a given lock is of French or English manufacture. There is a possibility, on the other hand, that perhaps the presence of three "French" features may eventually prove to have significance in placing the country of origin.

The following list indicates the characteristics and variations which can be expected to appear with some degree of success when examining a flintlock which has been archaeologically recovered.

1. Lockplate proper
    A. Length
    B. Width
    C. Cross section
        (1) Flat with beveled edges
        (2) Rounded (plano-convex)
    D. Bottom edge
        (1) With pronounced curve
        (2) With moderate curve
        (3) Straight
    E. Mainspring ledge, length
    F. Lockscrew holes
        (1) Two or three
        (2) Location of center hole
            a. In mainspring ledge
            b. Behind mainspring ledge
    G. Frizzen spring screw hole
        (1) Hidden
        (2) Exposed
2. Flashpan
    A. Rounded
    B. Pronounced "V" shape
    C. Flat "V"
    D. Pan removable from lockplate
    E. Pan integral with lockplate
3. Frizzen
    A. Straight
    B. Curved
    C. Bridled
    D. Not bridled

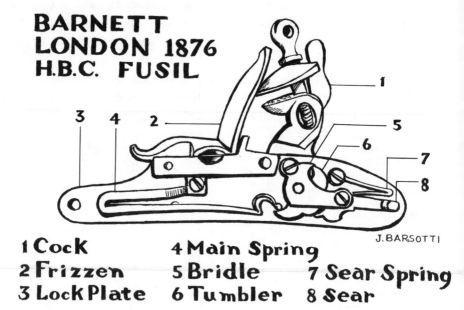

BARNETT LONDON 1876 H.B.C. FUSIL

J. BARSOTTI

1 Cock   4 Main Spring

2 Frizzen   5 Bridle   7 Sear Spring

3 Lock Plate   6 Tumbler   8 Sear

Figure 70. Illustration showing the various parts of a flintlock.
Drawn for this publication by John Barsotti.

4. Frizzen spring
    A. Notched for bridle link
    B. Not notched for bridle link
    C. Frizzen spring screw
        (1) Hidden
        (2) Exposed
5. Tumbler
    A. Bridled
    B. Not bridled
6. Cocks
    A. Type of comb
    B. Base
        (1) Flat face with beveled edges
        (2) Curved face (plano-convex in cross section)
    C. General curvature
    D. Late military type (double neck)

At first glance the above check list of flintlock characteristics appears rather forbidding. However, when the meaning behind it is understood, it is neither complex nor awkward.

In figures 71 and 72 are shown lockplate outlines. There is no better way to understand how the outline of the lockplate was changed during a 200 year period than to study these two illustrations. With these well in mind, one can date a lockplate within about 25 years of its actual time of manufacture with reasonable assurance.

At this point it also would be well to re-examine the drawing by John Barsotti (Fig. 70) showing the names of the various flintlock parts, which will be constantly used in this report.

The term "bridled" frizzen or tumbler requires some explanation. When the flintlock was originally invented in the early 1600's, the cock and tumbler assembly rotated on only one bearing; the hole in the lockplate. Consequently, when at full bent ("full cock" in modern parlance), the mainspring bore down on the tumbler, causing it to rub below the hole while the cock rubbed against the lockplate above the hole. This friction slowed down the action of the lock and reduced its efficiency. By about 1700, this fault in design was being corrected by extending a plate over the unsupported side of the tumbler, and having a pin in the tumbler bear in a hole in this supporting plate. In this way the tumbler was supported on both sides and rotated freely, without excessive friction. The supporting plate is known as the "tumbler bridle", and a tumbler so supported is a "bridled tumbler".

The frizzen on the original flintlocks was mounted by simply pivoting the frizzen on a screw threaded into the lockplate. The hammering of the cock on the frizzen, as well as the bumps received in normal use, often bent this screw slightly and slued the frizzen to one side. This fault was finally corrected by extending a support for the head from the frizzen screw from either the outer edge of the flashpan or from the frizzen spring screw. This form of frizzen bridle, which is little more than a flat link extending from one screw head to the other, is a feature of the French model 1717 military musket. (Fig. 78A). The frizzen bridle which is an integral part of the flashpan is the more advanced form of the two, and also the more effective.

Both the bridled tumbler and the bridled frizzen were in use on best grade guns by the end of the first quarter of the 18th Century. Therefore, if you know that the lock in question was of high quality, the presence or absence of bridles can be relied upon as a dependable clue to its age. Unfortunately, single isolated locks found in archaelogical excavations can seldom be assumed to be of any particular quality since the weathering and rust of the centuries makes it impossible to judge the original skill of the workman.

If the lock conforms to well established trade gun types, well and good. Nevertheless there is always the possibility that the gun was taken from some explorer or trader and was an exceedingly high grade firearm. When dealing with 17th and 18th Century archaeologically recovered flintlocks one cannot escape feeling that some of them are of better quality than is ordinarily assumed. Therefore, in assigning tentative dates to flintlocks one should be guided more by the general outline of the lockplate than by the presence or absence of bridles.

The cocks found on these Indian sites also have great diagnostic possibilities. Figure 73, shows important differences developed during the 17th Century. The comb is of special significance. The serpentine cock had become broad and flat, as in No's. 5E and 6F, Figure 18, page 48, with a groove set vertically in its face. By the late 1700's the comb had narrowed down again, as it had been originally in the first half of the preceding century. (See Figure 17, cocks no. 1A, 2B, and 3C.)

In writing of these evolutionary changes in locks, lockplates, and cocks there is always the danger of oversimplification. Actually nothing is clear cut; what applies in one instance may not apply in another. Most decisions are tentative; such as the shape of flashpans, or new improvements, the bridled tumbler or frizzen, were often adopted by other locksmiths as quickly as they were seen. But, again, these new improvements may have been ignored by other locksmiths in the same city for fifty or more years.

International boundaries offered no obstruction whatever to the interchange of new concepts in gun construction. So far, at least, no feature, or combinaton of features, has been isolated which can be relied upon to indicate that a particular lock is either "French" or "English." Therefore, some system, or systems, of identification, other than that of inspection, must be developed.

One possibility is that of metallurgical analysis. However, this process is expensive and archaeological budgets are exceedingly slim. In spite of this, there is a definite possibility that some progress may be made along that line of inquiry soon. In the meantime, there appears to be very little literature available on the subject; the most complete summary is by Robert B. Gordon, entitled *"Early Gunsmith's Metals"*[1].

A more direct method, and one which has been gratifyingly successful in a number of instances, is to process the lockplate in such a way as to read the lettering or date originally stamped upon the plate by the smith. This is not as fantastic a proposition as it sounds, but one must not expect more from the process than it can produce.

In the first place, not all lockplates were obligingly marked by the maker with his name or the date of manufacture. In the second, it is more difficult to bring out markings which were engraved than those stamped into the metal. The third difficulty is that no two pieces of ancient iron, even when from the same site, seem to rust in the same way. Some are not too corroded by rust while others have deep rust pocks, and it has so far been found impossible to read lockplates whose surfaces are badly eroded. Gooding, in Canada, and Maxwell, at Michilimackinac, have had excellent results using the caustic soda and etching processes repectively, [Explained pp. 213-223].

The caustic soda process described by Gooding on page 221, is technically known as the *electrochemical method* because it depends upon electrolytic action. A variation of that method, as used by the Smithsonian Institution, will be found on page 219. Actually, it is used primarily to clean the iron object of all rust flakes and, in that way, stop further deterioration of iron artifacts. Unless thoroughly cleaned, they continue to rust by picking up moisture from the atmosphere. The only way to stop this is to remove all traces of rust and then saturate the iron object with melted paraffin. From this it can be seen that success of the electrochemical method in making markings legible depends upon uniform rusting of both the surface and the bottom of the stamp-

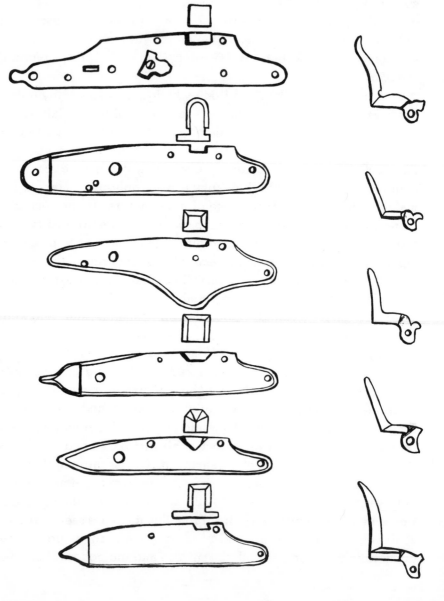

Figure 71. Lockplate outlines.

From FLINTLOCKS OF THE IROQUOIS, 1620-1687, by Joseph R. Mayer, (plate 3, page 40). Reproduced through the courtesy of the author and the Rochester Museum of Arts and Sciences. Descriptions after Dr. Mayer.

Lockplates, beginning at top:
1. From an early English dog lock. Plate has flat surface and edges. Above is an outline drawing of the undersurface of the pan. 1620-1640.
2. A long, heavy, flat lockplate with a beveled tail. Note method of keying pan to plate. From a dog lock, 1640-1660.
3. Plate from a flintlock showing striking similarities to those of the wheel lock. It is forged flat with beveled edges. Note shape of pan. 1630-1650.
4. A distinct form of lockplate. The surface is flat, the edges beveled, and the tail chamfered and drawn out to a long nipple-like finial. 1640-1660.
5. A later style also forged flat with beveled margins. We are here approaching the conventional 18th Century form. Note five facets on lower surface of pan. 1660-1680.
6. Another late 17th Century form still showing flat surface with beveled edges. Tail is chamfered and pointed. Flashpan is shown detached and in its entirety in order to show how strongly it was keyed to the plate. 1680-1700.

Frizzens, beginning at top:
A. Frizzen, double curved, from lockplate similar to No. 3 above. 1630-1650.
B. Straight frizzen, 1660-1680.
C. Slightly curved frizzen from lock similar to No. 4 above. 1640-1660.
D. Straight frizzen, 1650-1690.
E. A large, boldly curved frizzen similar to those of the 18th Century. However, it came from a lock of the 1640-1660 period.

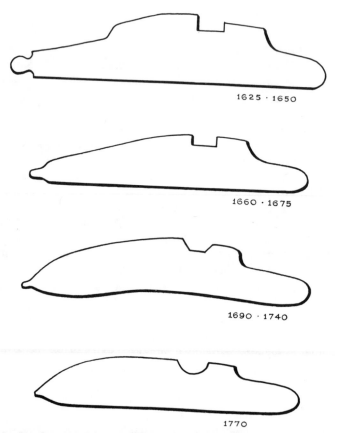

1625 · 1650

1660 · 1675

1690 · 1740

1770

Figure 72. Outlines of lockplates showing the general trend in the evolution of the flintlock from about 1625-1770.

From ARMS AND ARMOUR IN COLONIAL AMERICA by Harold L. Peterson. Reproduced through the courtesy of the author and the Stackpole Company.

ing or engraving. By carefully removing the overlying rust so as not to mar the underlying surface, the letter or date is revealed.

A closely related method of reducing rust in which an electric current and an electrolytic bath is used, is described in page 223.

The acid etching method of raising obliterated markings seems to work only where the marks have been actually stamped into the metal. After the iron has been cleaned by either the electrochemical or the electrolytic bath, and no markings can be made out, the acid etching solution should be tried. Needless to say, extreme caution must be exercised in preparing the surface for etching, since the deeper the grinding the less likelihood there is of bringing out the markings.

Moreau S. Maxwell was given some gunlocks for study which had been recovered at Michilimackinac about fifty years ago. Upon removing the overlying rust he found the under surface deeply pocked and in much worse condition than those excavated just the year before. From his description, the locks found at Michilimackinac some fifty years ago are in the same condition as those which have been found in Missouri. None of the Missouri locks are recent finds. The ones from the Gunsmith's Cache have also been out of the ground for about fifty years, while the locks from the Osage villages have been in storage for at least thirty.

From combined experiences it appears that iron objects left in the ground eventually achieve some sort of an equilibrium with the rusting process. To remove these same objects from the ground and store them under cover, but without cleaning the surfaces of all rust and sealing them from atmospheric moisture, upsets this equilibrium and accelerates oxidation under the individual rust flakes. This increased activity in the rusting process under the individual rust flakes produces the rust pocks which make it impossible to recover any of the markings so necessary in indentification.

It follows, then, that if one is not equipped to clean iron objects immediately, the best place to store them is in the ground where they were found until such time as proper care can be taken of them.

1. Gordon, Robt. B. (1959) "Early Gunsmith's Metal", AMERICAN RIFLEMAN, December, pp. 32-34.

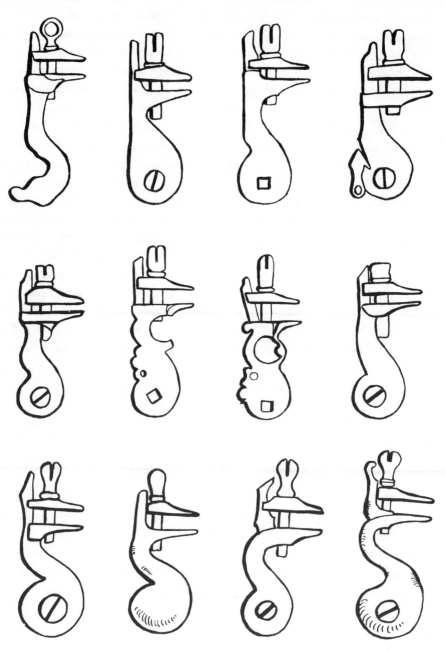

Plate 2

Top Row   A   B   C   D
Middle Row   E   F   G   H
Bottom Row   I   J   K   L

Figure 73. Twelve characteristic cock types found on 17th Century Seneca Sites.

Roughly they present an evolutionary series covering the entire century.

A. Cock from early dog lock of 1620-1640 period.

B. Undoubtedly a primitive form as suggested by the rigid body and neck, period 1640-1660.

C. In this cock a notch at the rear begins to differentiate the base from the neck, period 1640-1660.

D. A dog lock cock of the 1640-1660 period. Dog is also shown to illustrate how it acted as safety.

E. An unusual variety with a double curved neck, 1640-1660.

F. This form seems to have developed from the former (E). The reinforcements (now partially lost) are highly decorative, 1640-1660.

G. This is obviously an elaboration of F, period also 1640-1660.

H. A distinguished form with small base, tall slightly curved neck and highly placed flint-vise, period 1640-1660.

I. In general form this is similar to H. However, all features are fully developed. The body is large and the curve of the neck sharp. This cock begins to acquire the characteristics of the gooseneck type, period 1660-1680.

J. In outline this resembles the previous cock. It is distinguished, however, by an oval surface and the absence of a hole for the attachment to the tumbler shaft. In this specimen the hammer if forged to the shaft and attachment to the tumbler made within the lock, period 1660-1690.

K. Here for the first time we encounter the familiar gooseneck cock. As seen, the neck curves backward and then abruptly forward to become integrated both in design and stucture with the lower jaw of the flint vise. The tang, although forged in one piece with the cock, appears to emerge from the top of the lower jaw of the flint vise, period 1660-1680.

L. This is the typical oval faced gooseneck cock of 1680-1700.

From FLINTLOCKS OF THE IROQUOIS, 1620-1687, by Joseph R. Mayer, (plate 2, page 38). Reproduced through the courtesy of the author and the Rochester Museum of Arts and Sciences. Descriptions after Dr. Mayer.

[Chapter 15]
CLEANING METAL
The Recovery of Markings
by
T.M. Hamilton

All iron objects found in normal archaeological work have been subjected to rust attack. In some instances the rust has merely formed a protective coating on the surface and the markings are still easily read. The three Northwest locks described by Hanson (pp. 107-114) illustrate this fortunate circumstance. The locks found in the Gunsmith's Cache (see chapter 4) are examples of advanced corrosion. They are not only deeply pocked, but many of the lockplates are covered with rust scales. If one of these scales is pried off and the under surface examined with a glass of moderate magnification, small beads of moisture can be seen. Even though these lockplates are kept in a relatively dry room, the rust scales still absorb moisture from the atmosphere and the rusting process, if allowed to proceed unchecked, will eventually reduce the entire lockplate to a solid mass of rust. Of course, under museum conditions this will take years to accomplish, but the fact remains that all iron objects, if not too badly corroded when found, should be freed from the coating of rust and the surface then sealed so that additional moisture cannot be absorbed from the surrounding atmosphere.

Of course, if the object has been completely reduced to rust, the attack has run its course, and there is no iron core to be salvaged. Also, it must be borne in mind that often, when the overlying coat of rust has been removed, distressingly little of the iron core will be left and it would have been better to have been left in its original state. At least then, with its heavy coating of rust, it still approximated its original shape and was much more useful for study, even though it was doomed to eventual total destruction. For a more detailed and authoritative discussion of this particular problem consult Plenderleith.[1]

There are two accepted methods used in removing the corrosive products on iron, copper, or brass; both of which are electrolytic in action. In one, known as the *electrochemical* the object to be treated is surrounded by zinc, placed in a glass or earthenware dish, and covered with a caustic soda solution. Without the use of batteries or wiring, an electrolytic action is automatically induced between the zinc and the metal core beneath the corrosion; the corrosive products being transferred from the object to be cleaned to the surfaces of the surrounding zinc.

By way of contrast, in the *electrolytic* process we actually utilize an electroplating system. An electrical power source of approximately twelve volts is required. Whether this is furnished by a rectifier or a couple of six volt storage batteries in series is immaterial so long as it is direct current. A rheostat of some sort to control the amperage, an ammeter, and a suitable tank containing a caustic soda solution complete the setup. In this process, the metal object to be cleaned is attached to the negative terminal and becomes the cathode, while the iron plate suspended in the solution is attached to the positive terminal and acts as the anode. By properly adjusting the current flow, the corrosive products are thereby transferred from the surface of the object to the surface of the iron plate. Detailed instructions on both of these systems will be found at the end of this article. (See, also, Plenderleith in bibliography.)

Once the object has been properly freed from rust, its surfaces must be protected from further attacks induced by moisture absorbed from the atmosphere. The Smithsonian Institution recommends lacquer, but Gooding simply immerses the object in very hot paraffin and lets it drain. Because of the obvious dangers involved in using heated lacquer, though the paraffin probably does not leave as clean a surface, it is much safer to use and hence preferable.

The fact that Gooding has been able to read the markings on lock plates after cleaning them by the electrochemical process indicates one of two possibilities; either (1) the conditions of the soil and water in which the objects were found were such that they merely induced a beneficial, or protective, coating of rust over the iron surfaces, or (2) they produced a uniform rusting of both the surface of the iron and the bottom of the letters stamped or engraved in that surface so that little disturbance resulted in the relationship between the two.

Maxwell, in working with the lockplates from Michilimackinac,[2] which was occupied by the French from about 1715 to 1761 and by the

British from 1761 to 1781, has apparently had to contend with rust which has advanced to a more destructive stage than that found by Gooding, but still relatively mild when compared with the usual condition of the Osage lockplates found in Missouri. Consequently, in order to read the markings on his lockplates—and Maxwell has been astonishingly successful in doing so—he has had to resort to additional steps.

Maxwell uses a variation of the police technique of raising obliterated markings which have been ground off guns or motor blocks to avoid identification. This technique is based upon the fact that a punch mark stamped into the surface of a piece of metal, deforms the molecules of metal immediately beneath the punch or die mark. By polishing this surface and then treating it with an acid solution, the underlying metal is etched and the original letters or numbers can be read even though the original depression caused by the die has been completely removed.

The procedure followed, naturally, varies, but if the surface where the markings lay is irregular from being beaten or filed, it is smoothed with emery cloth, care being taken not to remove any more of the metal than absolutely necessary. Though the surface need not be polished down until it is absolutely glass-smooth, according to the police instructions, the fact still remains that the better the polish, the greater your chances of eventually reading the marking. The etching solution suggested by the Bureau of Standards is as follows:

4 parts, by weight, copper ammonium chloride
48 parts, by volume, hydrochloric acid
48 parts, by volume, distilled water

The etching solution is first applied cold, using a plain cotton swab. Do not expect instant results. Sometimes it requires the expenditure of much time, energy, and patience before the markings begin to appear. Occasionally, it has taken several hours of etching.

If the etching does not raise the numbers, the metal can be heated. In fact, the use of the acid and heat can be alternated, if thought desirable. As in tempering by heat colors, a good polish is almost essential when attempting to raise numbers by heating the metal. If the marking does not make its appearance by the time the metal has reached the red stage, there is no point in continuing.

Maxwell follows a slightly different system. His comments are as follows:

"The system I have been using is to first grind the surface of the lockplate with a fine-grain stone on a small, hand-held Roto-tool, usually finishing with a polishing bit. This first step is really the most effective. A good bit of the engraving will show up below the level of polished steel, and of course, the letters if they are deeply stamped. If the letters are unreadable, or if there is no visible marking on the plate ahead of the hammer, or at either end, I then resort to the acid. The following are the formulae the Michigan State Police use:

1—for soft metals—
Copper Chloride ½ oz.
Wood (methol) alcohol 1 oz.
Hydrochloric Acid 1 oz.
2—for iron and steel—
Copper Ammonium chloride ½ gr.
Distilled water 16 cc
Dissolve and add 8 cc concentrated HCl

"Actually, I use the two formulae interchangeably—if one doesn't work, I try the other. The police use these solutions by fastening wires to plus and minus ends of a flashlight battery, fastening one end to the metal to be tested, and the other to a cotton swab which is dipped in the solution and spread on the metal. I usually just hold the lockplate moistened with acid over the alcohol lamp. I then neutralize the plate, and flush it with water, and have found that if I put the lockplate under a low-power microscope with plenty of water still on it I can see more than if the plate is dried. If something is stamped in the metal I have been able to read it (eventually) in all cases."[3]

From the above it is obvious that success in reading the markings on lockplates is directly proportional to the patience expended. The greatest danger is that everyone at first expects too much in the way of results. Maxwell states "the only time I have actually gotten a textbook example of etching is on a French knife in which the letters had been pounded very deeply. Most of it is going back to the microscope time after time trying to make out another letter..."[4]

If Maxwell's letter is interpreted correctly, he has actually succeeded in reading thirteen lockplates out of a total of sixteen.[5]

As has been said, the majority of the lockplates from the Osage sites in Missouri have been so badly eroded by rust that the present surface, after the cleaning process is complete, is so far below the original surface of the metal that there is little possibility that the lettering can ever be raised. However, in some instances the rusting has been confined to pockets which have produced sharply defined pocks separated by areas of metal relatively untouched by rust. The explanation for this is that those lockplates on whose surfaces the rust pocks have not yet enlarged to the point where they are joined together continuously were either made of a better iron or were lodged in a more neutral soil.

By carefully grinding the rust from the surface of these better preserved lockplates with a 180 grit wheel, and then swabbing them with the etching acid, there appeared to be part of letters on three separate lockplates. Additional grinding and swabbing eventually resulted in making out enough of the letter forms between the pocks to read the name "Barnett", and in one instance the date, "1805."

Now, the following must be clearly understood. When working with badly eroded iron, the name as it was originally stamped will never be read. All one can ever hope to see are enough fragments of the lettering to identify the name. For instance, on the most successful lock the final lettering read "P PNETT". The rust pocks had removed the lower parts on a "B" and an "R", and completely obliterated the "A" of the original mark—"BARNETT". On the 1805 Barnett lock, the number "5" could be made out quite distinctly, but only the right half of the "0" could be seen, the "18" was completely missing. However the "1805" reading was justified simply because common sense dictates that it could have been neither a "17" nor a "19". On another lock the lettering, as it finally developed appeared something like this: "NFTT". Because of its position across the tail of the plate, it was obvious that there was room ahead of these letters for the missing "BAR" and that the "F" was actually an "E" with the lower bar missing.

In addition to patience, a good imagination is necessary and as complete a list of old gunsmiths as can be found. For instance, in the Nebraska State Historical Museum is to be found lockplate No. 1569. Beneath the pan are three word fragments, one above the other. The first line reads "WOCILE". Beneath it are the letters "SARGAN", and beneath them are the letters "SCRA". Probably, the second name is "Sargant", though the only gunsmiths of that period were the "Sargent Brothers. The bottom name is probably "Scranton". However, what "WOCILE" represents is not known.

The abstract from Plenderleith on electrolytic reduction, and the summaries on the electrochemical method by Gooding and Elder which follow will be found most useful.

1. Plenderleith, H.J. (1956) THE CONSERVATION OF ANTIQUITIES AND WORKS OF ART, London.
2. Maxwell, Moreau S. (1959) Archaeological Investigation of Fort Michilimackinac, Preliminary Report, (Hectograph), The Museum, Michigan State Univ., East Lansing.
3. Maxwell, (18 Jan. 1960) Personal Letter.
4. ibid.
5. ibid.

THE ELECTROCHEMICAL METHOD*

Many iron objects which have come from excavations have undergone major chemical change which will eventually result in their complete destruction if steps are not taken to counteract it and seal the object from the effects of moisture in the air. Following are the steps in the order of their use for this work.

1. By physical means—either hammer or wire brush, depending on the nature of the object, remove part of the heavy incrustation. Also, bare one spot of solid iron so that the electrolytic process will not be hindered in its need for contact with the solid original form.

2. The container for the process should preferably be enamel, or stoneware, not less than glazed pottery, and not glass because the expansion force of the chemical action will usually break it. If any material is used other than enamel, it is better to use a flaring-sided bowl rather than a vertical sided one, because this reduces the breaking effect of the expansion force. Place in the vessel a layer of *thin zinc chips,* * on top of which specimens are laid out separately and covered with another layer of zinc chips. This may be repeated to fill the vessel, just leaving room for the liquid to thoroughly cover it.

3. Make a 5 percent (instead of 20 percent, which is for the quicker method) solution of sodium hydroxide (caustic soda) and cover the materials in the vessel. (Sodium hydroxide is ordinary household lye.)

4. This will take about 6 weeks in the chemical bath. However, to achieve maximum effect, when the visible action (bubbling) has stopped in about one week, which means that the zinc has been used up, the specimens must be taken out and separated from the zinc around them by washing in dilute sulphuric acid and then in clear water before returning them to a new zinc and sodium hydroxide bath. This needs to be done because when chemical action has stopped the zinc coating around the specimen will prevent further effect. Therefore this needs to be repeated several times until it appears that the suface of the specimens has lost its rusted nature and is fairly solid iron.

5. When the specimen is taken out for the final time it will have a white coating of zinc which is to be removed first almost in its entirety by a bath in dilute nitric acid and possibly by a small amount of wirebrushing or picking of loose flakes. The acid bath is of course to be followed by a good washing in clear water, after which it must be

thoroughly dried, in an oven if available, otherwise, just air dried in the sun, etc.

6. The final treatment of a preservative coating which must then be applied to prevent further chemical deterioration by rusting is best in the form of lacquer. This may be applied by spraying or with a brush, but is best done by immersing the specimen in a pan of lacquer placed in a double boiler and bringing this to a low boil for about a half hour. This last method gives better results, because the lacquer penetrates the irregularities of the material and leaves the specimen with a better appearance; that is, the coating shows less than when it is brushed on. The boiling should be very light, really just a simmer, and it should be done carefully in a well ventilated room because the lacquer is very inflammable.

*Furnished through the courtesy of Mr. R.A. Elder, Jr., Ass't. Curator, Division of Ethnology, Smithsonian Institution. Refer to: Lee G. Crutchfield, "Chemical Preparation and Preservation of Museum Antiquities," Museum News, 15 Jan. 1937, P. 7-8, of which the following is a variation, in some respects found to be useful.

*Bought as "mossy zinc". [Another good method is to melt the zinc and pour it into cold water. This is an easy way to clean up used zinc referred to in paragraph 4.

THE ELECTROCHEMICAL REDUCTION
by
S. James Gooding

The electrochemical reduction of the corrosive products of iron and bronze can be accomplished with very little equipment. The object is placed in a glass dish completely covered (or wrapped, depending upon the form of the zinc) with zinc granules, zinc wool or zinc strips cut from light weight sheets. Zinc granules or wool are easier to use but are not always available. The object is then covered with a 10 to 20 percent solution of commercial flake caustic soda dissolved in water. This is allowed to remain until reaction ceases. The object is then removed from the zinc and brushed under running water. It may be necessary to repeat the process two or three times using fresh materials. The caustic soda is extremely dangerous and should not be allowed to touch the skin. When the desired degree of reduction has been obtained, the object should be very thoroughly washed in running water for two or three days and should then be checked to determine if all the chlorides have been removed! When dry, the object may be immersed in melted paraffin wax to prevent further absorption of moisture.

1. Plenderleith, H.J., (1956) The Conservation of Antiquities and Works of Art, London, pp. 197-199.

THE ELECTROLYTIC REDUCTION

Equipment

Select a glass tank of suitable size and shape. Make up a 5 percent solution of caustic soda (1 oz. of household lye per pint of water) and pour in tank. Provide a D.C. electric supply of 12 volts (two 6 volt storage batteries in series). A rheostat to control the amperage will be needed. Also some wire and iron plates to use as anodes.

If a galvanized iron tank must be used in place of the glass, run current until all galvanizing has been removed. Throw away the solution and start over fresh.

Procedure

The corroded object acts as the cathode. The current should be about 10 amps per square decimeter of cathode area if the corroded object is of iron. Copper and silver must be kept above 2 amps or a black deposit will be made on the object.

Then attach corroded object to negative pole of power supply (the cathode). Use iron plates a few inches distant as the anodes.

Anodes must be removed from time to time and brushed free of slag which gathers on them. Also brush off specimen.

Remove object while current is on. Do not shut off current and leave object in the tank or it will be plated with metallic impurities in the solution.[1]

A simplified version of the electrolytic system for removing iron oxides appeared in the May-June, 1959, issue of GRIST, a publication of the National Park Service. This particular set up was devised by Robert Stevens at Fort Frederica, and utilized a 12 volt storage battery charger for the power supply. An ammeter was improvised by introducing a hanging coil of ordinary stove pipe wire into the circuit and clipping one of the charger leads to this wire to control the resistance. A 5 percent solution of caustic soda was used.

1. Plenderleith, op. cit., pp. 194-197.
2. Stevens, Robt. (1959) GRIST, National Park Service.

[Chapter 16]
INVESTIGATING THROUGH X–RAY
by
Carl P. Russell

In the summer of 1957, Edward Morse discovered the butt of a gun protruding from the sand and gravel in the bed of the Hoback River in Western Wyoming. He pulled it out and found that apparently the relic was an entire gun, lacking only the buttplate. It was encrusted with cemented sand and pebbles in such manner as to obscure most of its significant parts. Only the buttstock remained free from the compact cover.

Young Morse carried his find to the Superintendent of the near-by Grand Teton National Park who advised that the gun should be examined in the museum laboratories of the National Park Service. The finder of the gun agreed to lend it for study and ultimate exhibit in the Moose Visitor Center, Grand Teton National Park.

When the specimen reached the museum laboratories in Washington, D.C., technicians there decided to leave the remarkable encrustation intact and to investigate the hidden mechanism by means of X-ray pictures. The result of this inquiry into the identity of the piece is indicated in the accompanying drawings.

Obviously, the gun is a flintlock trade musket of the characteristic "North West Gun" class. The internal lock mechanism has little definition in the X-ray and has been omitted in the drawing, but the external lock parts show clearly enough. The "one screw only, which passes quite through the stock, and secures the upper [forward] part of the trigger guard to the lower part [breech tang] of the barrel," as specified in 1809 by the U.S. Indian Trade Office[1] is clearly in evidence. Many makers of trade guns passed this long screw through

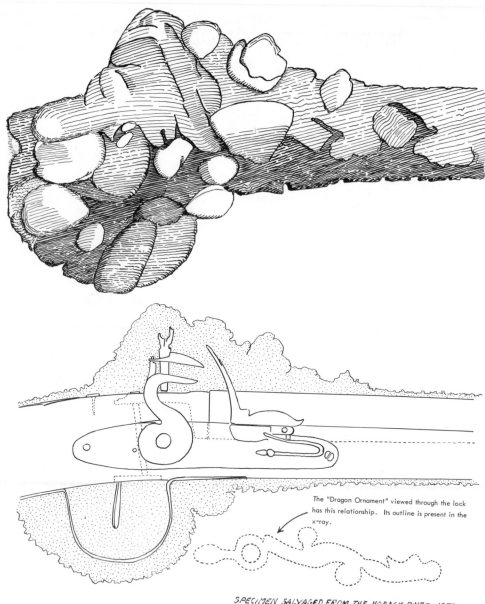

The "Dragon Ornament" viewed through the lock has this relationship. Its outline is present in the x-ray.

SPECIMEN SALVAGED FROM THE HOBACK RIVER 1957
GRAND TETON NATL. PARK COLLECTIONS, MOOSE, WYO.

ENCRUSTED TRADE GUN X-RAYED

Figure 74. Two views of the Hoback River Gun found by Edward Morse.

The upper sketch shows encrustation of cemented sand and pebbles completely covering lock and trigger guard. The lower sketch shows the gun construction as revealed by X-ray. Drawn for this publication by Carl P. Russell.

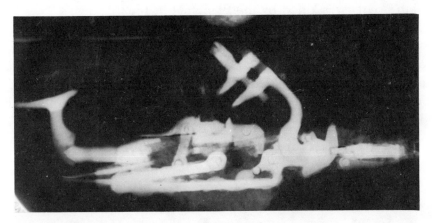

Figure 75. Photograph and X-ray of Gun Lock.

Another excellent example of the use of X-ray in studying archaeological gun parts
heavily encrusted with rust. A snaphaunce lock from grave 93, Power House Site,
Lima, N.Y. Apparently this lock was discarded because the cover to the pan no longer
opened when the cock was tripped, for the cock is down, but the pan is still covered.
In the X-ray the thrust link from cock to pan cover is disconnected at the pan end.
From the Harry L. Schoff collection. Photos courtesy of Mr. Schoff.

the stock in such a manner as to connect with the trigger guard immediately in front of the bow. In the Hoback specimen it connects with a plate which fits just behind the bow. Certain unidentified makers in Belgium did this, as did Hollis, Wheeler, Sargent Brothers and probably others in England.

The traditional "Dragon Ornament" in the X-ray is obscured by the lock mechanism behind which it falls, but the greater part of its outline can be seen. As the drawing indicates, it is the typical brass "Dragon" which, as a sideplate, marked such trade guns of any and all makes during the 18th and 19th Centuries.

In the region of the grip several tacks appear, only one of which is shown in the drawing. Probably they held a patch of rawhide, wrapped around the grip and nailed to the wood while wet, to strengthen the broken or cracked stock—a common practice of both Indians and mountain men in making repairs in the field. Numerous trade guns now in collections show this type of mending.

It is idle to attempt to link this relic with a specific fight, but it is a fact that it was found near the place where H.G.O. More (or Moore) of Wyeth's party was killed by the Blackfoot in 1832.

The Western Museum Laboratory of the National Park Service has devised a special exhibit featuring this relic in the history museum at Moose. It serves to point out some of the mechanical features of a trade gun, demonstrates the effectiveness of X-ray technique in identification and gives some emphasis to the idea of violence encountered by men, red and white, on the fur traders' frontier.

Released with the approval of Frank Oberhansley, Superintendant, Grand Teton National Park, in 1960, and Ralph Lewis, Chief of Museums, National Park Service, in 1960.

1. Letter Book, Superintendent of Indian Trade, Georgetown, D.C., May 12, 1809. Quoted in Russell, GUNS ON THE EARLY FRONTIERS, 1957, p. 106.

[Chapter 17]
THE IDENTIFICATION OF UNMARKED GUNLOCKS
by
R.T. Huntington

Unmarked gunlocks by themselves, without the remainder of the gun, present many serious problems to the researcher. The identification of an unknown gun involves many factors: style, material of stock and metal parts, and decoration, to name a few. No one feature can be depended on to determine with accuracy the date and place of manufacture; not even the wood of the stock. Although an American or European walnut stock might lead us to surmise as to the gun's origin, it is known that both types of wood were exported and used in other than their native areas. The stock material is merely one of several factors.

Considering the marked gunlock by itself, the problem is even more difficult. Assuming the lock to be in apparently original condition, it is possible to state that the lock is of a style used in a given country or during a more or less specific period. But how can it be proved that the lock was actually made at that time? The most that one could do after detailed study that included analysis of the metals used in its construction, would be to state that the lock's characteristics are (or are not) consistent with its production at a given time or place.

But this is very tentative. Although styles of cocks, frizzens, and the like differed from time to time and in various countries, the change is not uniform enough, even within a limited area, to be more than a rough guide. Thus, at a time when the gunsmiths of London and Paris may have been creating new styles, many country gunsmiths followed earlier trends; either because it was simpler to follow a pattern with which the gunsmith was familiar, or because their customers would

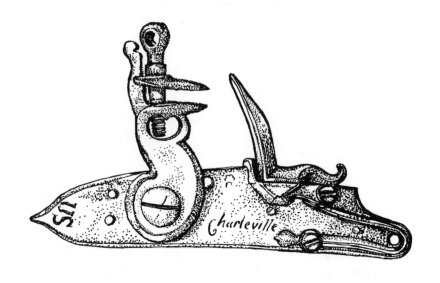

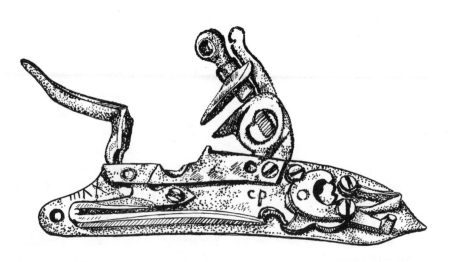

JOHN BARSOTTI
-1959-

Figure 76. Lock from a Model 1763 French Charleville flintlock musket.

The *U.S.* marking on the tail of the lockplate and *U.STATES* branded into the belly of the stock indicated service in the Continental Army during the American Revolution. The stock is decorated with fourteen old style brass tacks of the type commonly used in the Indian trade. *Drawn for this publication by John Barsotti.*

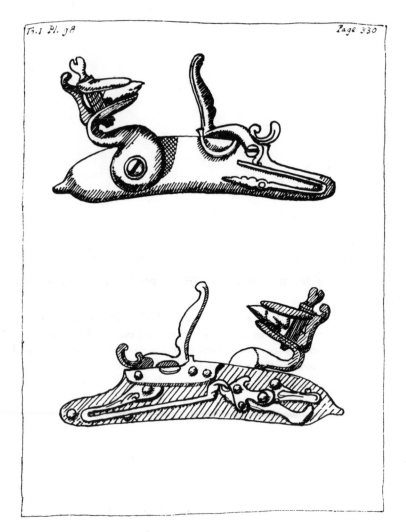

Figure 77. Lock of a French Military Musketoon late 17th Century.
(Military arms models had not yet been standardized.)
According to Saint Remy this lock mechanism found use not only in the musketoon, but also in the rifled carbine and in the pistol of the day.
MEMOIRES D'ARILLERIE, etc., Saint Remy, 1702, Amsterdam, reprinted by Major James E. Hicks, 1939. The illustration is from Plate 98, page 330, Vol. 1, redrawn for this publication by Carl P. Russell.

have no part of the new-fangled styles. Thus arms are found which were made at the same period whose styles differ by a half century or more. Example, wheellock arms were made as late as the 18th Century in Germany, just as Kentucky rifles can be ordered today. None of these facts makes the researcher's task any simpler.

If the lock has seen rough service, the darkness gets deeper. How can one tell which parts are original, and which are replacements? Only an educated guess can be made, from a comparison of the style of the parts. As noted, this is very uncertain business.

And what can be said of the early American gunsmith who saw an imported flintlock that appealed to him, and who proceeded to copy it? The French cock is beyond his capability, so he used a standard cock blank. He varied the style of the frizzen and pan to be somewhat more conservative. As for interior parts, there is no problem, and he used the same parts that he had used for the past twenty years. And he neglected to mark the lock with his name.

Time passes, and the lock is resurrected and sent to a museum for study. With no knowledge of the actual source of the lock, the expert cannot be censured if he concludes that this is a French-made lock made just as the new style was coming into flower, and that the cock is obviously a replacement.

These are some of the pitfalls. Now, what can be done?

The first step is to assemble, from as many sources as possible, data on locks whose origin is unquestioned. This should include both military and sporting types; not only those of the major arms producing areas, but of country makers—such as some of the Kentucky gunsmiths—as well. Then, study the material. For this purpose an outline sketch of the lockplate, cock, frizzen, pan tumbler, bridle, and mainspring are excellent, as the sketches can be compared even more easily than the locks themselves. With some 50 to 100 of these drawings, tentative conclusions as to features characteristic of a given style and period can be made. And, less conclusively, as to place of origin, since new styles in locks traveled swiftly between major arms centers, but spread more slowly into the hinterlands.

Workmanship, too, must be recognized as an important factor in identifying locks. Distinguishing between the top quality work of the master craftsman, the good quality work of the average skilled gunmaker, and the cheap, mass-produced locks made for trade is a must. The best quality locks will usually (but not always) include the latest styles and improvements; they may be from ten to twenty years ahead

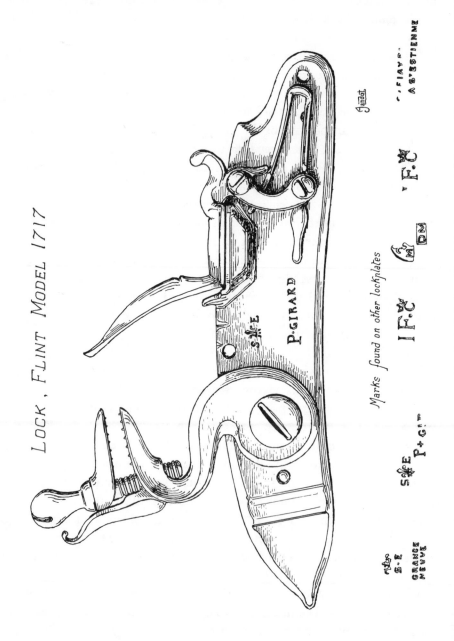

LOCK, FLINT MODEL 1717

P.GIRARD

S.t.E

Marks found on other lockplates

Janot

"FIAY"
A.S'ESTIENNE

'F.C

IF.C

DM

S.t.E
P+G.r

S.E
GRANGE
NEUVE

Figure 78 A&B. The French Model 1717 flintlock by Girard with illustrations of another 1717 lock and later models opposite.
Various proof marks are shown below the larger drawing. The 18th Century concept of standardization did not extend to uniformity, much less interchangability of parts. The various makers of the 1717 Model, for instance, filed their lockplates to suit their individual fancy, as is here shown. Indeed, there is some indication that lockplates made by the same locksmith for a given model would not always fit the same inletting. *Illustration from NOTES ON FRENCH ORDNANCE, 1717-1936 by James E. Hicks. Reproduced through courtesy of Major Hicks.*

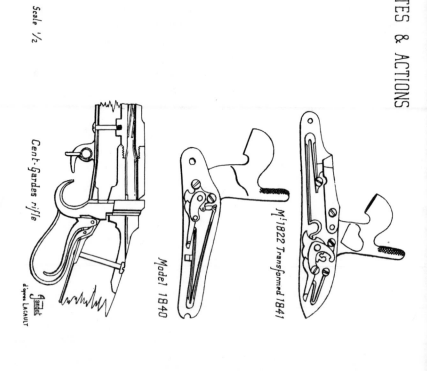

Model 1717

Model 1777

Model 1816-1822

Scale ½

Figure 78B.

LOCKPLATES & ACTIONS

M¹ 1822 Transformed 1841

Model 1840

Cent-Gardes rifle

d'après LACAULT

236

of the common run of locks in their design. On the other hand, the average good quality lock is likely to appear a bit old-fashioned in comparison with the 'dernier cri" of the fashionable maker. But it will be well-designed, with good workmanship, and probably will not be highly ornamented.

The cheap grade is not hard to identify. Superficially it may resemble a good lock; it may, indeed, even work well. The lockplate and cock may be coarsely engraved. But the poor fitting of parts, and the even rougher finish of the interior lock mechanism are revealing. Moreover, such locks frequently lack a bridle from the pan to the frizzen, and may not even have a bridle for the tumbler. At first glance the absence of these features might lead one to consider such a lock as being from a much earlier period than is actually the case; the overall styling, and, above all, the careless workmanship will usually suffice, though, to put such a lock in its proper place. Determining the period of manufacture of such a lock may be difficult, as such locks were made for export practically up to the present time, with very little, if any, change from the locks of a century ago.

Yet care must be taken to distinguish between the cheap trade lock and the frequently crude product of a frontier—or even an Indian—gunsmith, who worked with the simplest possible equipment. The difference is this: The mass produced lock was deliberately made as inexpensively as possible; parts are roughly made, rather than crude. File marks will be quite evident.

The frontier lock, on the other hand, may show evidence of hand forging or even forge welding of parts; there will probably be fewer file marks. The lock will be very simple, rather than cheaply constructed. Such a lock is, of course, of distinct historical value, since it testifies to the meager facilities available when it was made.

With these thoughts in mind, first try to segregate those locks that are quite obviously "trade locks" of the common class. Such locks would probably form a sizable portion of a gunsmith's stock for frontier trade . . . especially for Indian use. Next, the military locks. Recalling how frequently broken parts were replaced, identifying a lockplate alone may be all that can be accomplished, as no original internal parts may remain.

Finally, the many different locks, from one source or another—from broken guns, from arms having replaced locks, etc.—are far and away the most difficult to classify.

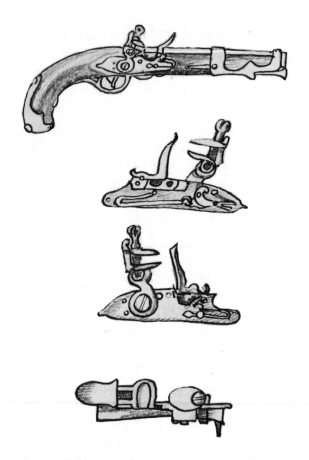

Figure 79. French Military pistol and its lock, 1766.
"This model was accepted for Cavalry, Dragoons and Hussars in 1766." *From water-color drawing by Col. Cirfontaine, 1789 (MS).*
The Cirfontaine manuscript is (or was) owned by the City Art Museum of St. Louis. Cirfontaine, Col. 1789. Dessins Relatis aux Travaux d'artillerie executes dans les manufactures, 1773-1789. (Manuscript text and original water color drawings. Never reproduced, so far as is known). The figures of the 1766 pistol are from plate 22 which is accompanied by longhand text. Copied for this publication by Carl P. Russell.

As to whether it is possible to determine with any degree of exactness the time and place that a specific gunlock—not attached to its original gun—was made, a regretful "no" must be given.

In general, it may be possible to classify locks into one of the categories described: it may be possible to say that a given lock is probably a trade lock of British origin. Others may be French, British, or American locks, or they may be copies: Their construction yields no clue. The only case in which a definite answer can be given is the rare instance when a lockplate of known military type turns up.

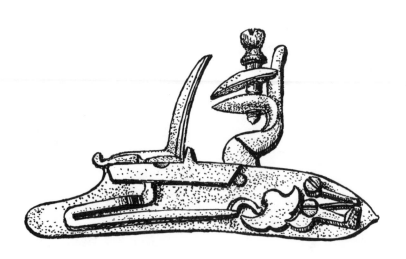

Figure 80. A plain grade of flintlock from an English fowling piece.
It was made without a bridle on either the tumbler or the frizzen. The frizzen spring has a roller, a refinement usually found on later locks or those of a better grade. *I. WALKER*, whose name is on the lockplate, was listed as a gunsmith at London in 1806 and Norwich, England, in 1832. Numerous gunsmiths named Walker were working in England during the 1770-1830 period.
Drawn for this publication by John Barsotti.

[Chapter 18]
DOCUMENTED DATES VERSUS DATES DERIVED FROM TRADE GOODS*
by
Carlyle S. Smith

Excavations carried on as part of the Inter Agency Archaeological Salvage Program in the Missouri Basin have frequently produced large amounts of goods manufactured in the United States or in Europe. Some of this material is derived from sites of military establishments occupied by the United States Army and some from aboriginal village sites.

Upon seeing the large number of gun parts, cartridge cases, bullets, and related items from the excavations of the State Historical Society of North Dakota at Like-a-Fishhook Village and of the Smithsonian Institution at Fort Stevenson, I volunteered my services in the identification of the specimens. Most of the data from Like-a-Fishhook Village were first published as appendices to manuscript reports on the site by James Howard and Alan Woolworth. Since that time an analysis was published.[1] The identification of the speciments from Fort Stevenson has been published in the PLAINS ANTHROPOLOGIST[2] and appeared as an appendix to the report on the site by G. Hubert Smith published by the Smithsonian Institution.

As the identification progressed I was struck by the remarkably close correlation between the documented dates for the sites and the dates assignable to the specimens. In conversation with colleagues on various occasions prior to this work I had tended to agree that dates derived from trade goods must be used with the utmost caution because any item manufactured within a well established date bracket could have been used much later. Such does not seem to be the case in the two sites under consideration here.

The first step in the identification was to sort the specimens on the basis of previous experience derived from collecting and studying antique firearms as a hobby. Tentative identifications were then checked against descriptions and illustrations in the literature, against specimens in various collections, and, in some instances, against opinions of other individuals with knowledge of the subject.

In the identification of parts of guns the literature was of little value because the illustrations usually depict only the completely assembled firearms and not the component parts. Knowledge acquired through handling and restoring hundreds of firearms was the best source of information. Cartridges were the items easiest to identify from the literature.

Like-a-Fishhook Village was established on a U-shaped bend of the Missouri River in Garrison County, North Dakota, by the Hidatsa in 1845. They were joined in the late 1850's by the Mandan. By 1862 the Arikara moved in, each tribe maintaining its separate area in the village. Trading posts were established also. As a result much of the aboriginal material culture disappeared in competition with artifacts made in the United States and Europe. The inhabitants were placed on individual allotments of land beginning in 1885 and the last earth lodge village on the Missouri River became an archaeological site.[3]

In the collection from Like-a-Fishhook Village the varieties of firearms range from the muzzle-loading flintlock trade musket (known as the Northwest Trade Gun) through muzzle-loading percussion guns and early breechloaders to semi-modern repeating rifles such as the Model 1873 Winchester. Revolvers are also represented. Cartridges range from experimental models made during the closing years of the Civil War to those made until some time prior to 1902.

The earliest possible date for the start of manufacture of a group of specimens is 1805. In his study of the flintlock Northwest Trade Gun,[4] Carl P. Russell has found 1805 to be the earliest date stamped on a specimen and 1876 to be the latest. In the collection from Like-a-Fishhook Village a lockplate from one of these guns bears the date 1885. Others marked "LEMAN" or "TRYON" date from about 1840. The date bracket for the Northwest Guns at the site is adjustable from 1805-1876 to about 1840-1876, on the basis of marked specimens.

The latest date obtainable from the specimens falls prior to 1902. This is based upon the occurrence of cartridges made by the Remington Arms Company and the Union Metallic Cartridge Company as separate organizations. After the two firms merged in 1902 the cartridges were marked REM-UMC. No cartridges bearing the later trade mark are present. Furthermore, there is no evidence the occupants of the site had guns that appeared as new models starting in 1886, or any that used smokeless powder, a commodity available after about 1890. The latest date that actually appears on a cartridge is 1883.

Between the extremes of 1840 and 1883 there are many specimens that furnish date brackets such as 1850-1865, 1861-1865, 1866-1868, 1868-1880. Some items bear dates accurate to the month: May 1879 and March 1880, for example. Documentation indicates that the site was occupied between 1845 and 1885, the mean date being 1865. The mean of all of the different dates derived from specimens is 1869. On the basis of the dates from the specimens alone it would be safe to assign the site to the last half of the 19th Century, or 1840 to 1890, to be more precise.

Fort Stevenson was established by the U.S. Army 19 miles from Like-a-Fishhook Village in 1867 and was abandoned as a military post in 1883. It served as one of the links in the chain of military posts protecting trail headed westward into Montana and eastward into Minnesota. In 1883 the buildings were turned over to the Bureau of Indian Affairs for use as a school[5]. At least one of the buildings was still standing in the late 1950's.

The identification of the specimens from Fort Stevenson presented a somewhat different problem from those found at Like-a-Fishhook Village because of the use of the site after 1883 as a school and the probable use of the buildings even later as temporary shelter for hunters and other visitors. After the initial sorting it was found that the specimens could be divided into two groups, one dating from the military occupation and the other from the civilian occupation.

Specimens assigned to the military occupation furnish 1855 as the earliest date and about 1900 as the latest date. Examples of dates falling between these two extremes are 1866-1880, 1868-1880, 1873-1890 and, specifically, June 1880, February 1881, April 1882. The mean date for the documentation of 1867 to 1883 is 1875. The mean date derived from the specimens is 1871. On the basis of the specimens alone it would be safe to assign the military occupation to about 1865-1885.

The specimens from the civilian occupation of the site indicate a range of from 1886 to 1951. Typical date brackets are 1887-1940 and from 1890, 1900, 1902, 1906, and 1913 to 1951, the year the site was excavated. The mean date for the civilian use of site, between 1883 and 1951, is 1917. The mean date derived from the specimens is 1920. On the basis of the specimens alone it would be safe to assume that the site has been in use in the period of about 1890-1950.

Aside from furnishing the near-equivalent to a controlled laboratory situation, in archaeology, the identification and dating of the objects from the two late sites are of importance in acculturation studies. It is interesting to note that the gun parts and cartridges from Like-a-Fishhook Village indicate that the Plains Indians of the last half of the 19th Century had far fewer repeating rifles and many more muzzle-loading smoothbore muskets than the writers of popular fiction would allow. Furthermore, the study offers confirmation of the sound conclusions drawn from research in documentary records by Parsons and du Mont in their study of the firearms used on both sides in the Battle of Little Bighorn.[6].

*A revision of a paper read at the annual meeting of the Society for American Archaeology, Bloomington, Ind., 7 May 1955.

1. Smith, Carlyle S. (1955) "An Analysis of the Firearms and Related Specimens from Like-A-Fishhook Village and Fort Berthold I" THE PLAINS ANTHROPOLOGIST, No.4.
2. _____, (1954) "Cartridges and Bullets from Fort Stevenson, North Dakota", THE PLAINS ANTHROPOLOGIST, No. 1, pp. 25-29.
3. Smith, G. Hubert (1957) "Archaeological Work at Like-A-Fishhook Village and Fort Berthold, Garrison Reservoir, North Dakota", THE PLAINS ANTHROPOLOGIST, No. 2.
4. Russell, Carl P. (1957) GUNS ON THE EARLY FRONTIER, pp. 103-130.
5. Mattison, Ray H. (1951) "Old Fort Stevenson, A Typical Missouri River Military Post", NORTH DAKOTA HISTORICAL QUARTERLY, Vol. 18, No. 2-3.
6. Parsons, John E. and John S. Du Mont (1953) FIREARMS IN THE CUSTER BATTLE.

IV

CONCLUSIONS

CONCLUSIONS
T.M. Hamilton

In reviewing the material so far presented it seems that there is enough information to justify a few hypotheses concerning the trade gun, its place in the fur trade, and its use by the Indian.

The first firearms offered the Indian in trade were probably surplus guns picked up from dealers in Europe. In the case of the Seneca, it was a smoothbore, either a wheellock or flintlock, of 16 gauge with a theoretical bore of about .662 inch. That was the standard military arm of the Dutch West Indian Company in 1655[1] and would accommodate the 17 gauge balls, with a nominal diameter of .650 inch, found on the Seneca sites. If and when bullets with a diameter of .73 inch are found (12 gauge) they will indicate the use of muskets with the standard bore of .775 inch of 10 gauge[2], and will suggest English rather than Dutch trade. However, it must be remembered that the Dutch were the only early 17th Century settlers who actually succeeded in standardizing their bores—12 gauge for matchlocks and 16 gauge for wheellock and flintlock arms.[3]

The lone .40 caliber bullet reported from the Washingtonboro site with an occupational date of 1600-1620 does not seem to fit in with any known smoothbores of that period, and was probably used as a buckshot rather than a ball. The fact that swan shot has also been found on that same site, strengthens this supposition. There is also the possibility that it might have been a rifle ball, either of that era or one much later. Also, we must not overlook the smoothbore barrel of .41 caliber found with the Gunsmith's Cache. Even though this barrel was of presumably later date than the .40 caliber ball, these exceedingly light guns may have enjoyed a greater and longer popularity than has been assumed.

249

By 1750, when the trade had penetrated to the Mississippi and beyond, firearms were being made specifically designed for the use of the Indian. Since he has always shown a decided preference for a gun of light weight, capable of handling shot as well as ball, it seems that the barrel fragments of .45, .50, and .53 caliber, found on the Osage sites of that period, represent the French attempt to cater to the demands of their customers. These guns of smaller bore were capable of killing the game normally encountered east of the Mississippi, and there is no reason to suppose that the French had any other intent than to comply with the demands of the trade.

However, upon crossing the Mississippi, where the buffalo, rather than the deer, became the chief meat animal upon which the Indian depended, the light French fusils were found to be unsatisfactory. It is estimated that in the 100 years preceding the French capitulation to the English in Canada over 200,000 trade guns had been made by the French factories.[4] Undoubtedly, some of these guns continued to be made for the trade in Louisiana after 1759 and the French gunmakers persisted in trying to find a market for their light calibered smoothbore long after the traders were finding them hard to sell in the face of the rising British competition. The need for a heavier ball brought about considerable experimenting during the closing years of the 18th Century and, by the time the 1800's were under way, the 24 gauge smoothbore was well established and remained the standard gauge until the close of the fur trade on the Plains.

In spite of the fantastic number of trade guns of French manufacture which went into the fur trade between 1650 and 1750, there is not one known example extant today. The only possible way we can know any details concerning it is to reconstruct it from the archaeological evidence. Presumably, the locks were indistinguishable from those of English manufacture. Until the beginning of the 1800's few had bridled frizzens or bridled tumblers. Since almost all guns of that period were full stocked, it is safe to assume that the French trade fusils were also. The lengths of barrel are unknown, but, assuming that the barrel fragments from the Osage sites are representative, it was octagonal in the breech, measuring an inch or more across the flats, and tapered down to a round midsection and muzzle. The bores were .45, .50, and .53 caliber; the middle size being by far the most popular. There is a definite possibility that .55 caliber, or 28 gauge, was also a favorite size among the French trade fusils, for almost as many of them are found on the Osage sites as the .50 caliber. However, there is the possibility that the 28 gauge guns were an intermediate step toward the final adoption of the 24 gauge.

Where barrel fragments of larger caliber are found in context with those of smaller, on 18th Century village sites, the probabilities seem to be that they were either from old military weapons introduced into the trade, or were originally the personal arms of white traders or explorers. All French military flintlocks from 1717 to 1836[5] had a standard bore of 17.5 mm., or .689 inch, except for the 1763 and 1766 Musketoons which had a bore of 17.1 mm. (.673 inch) and the carbines of 1793 with a bore of 13.5 mm. (.53 inch). The bore on the English Brown Bess was close to .75 inch, or 11 gauge, and the Committee of Safety usually specified that same bore when ordering muskets for the Colonies during the Revolution. It may be said that the English military muskets from the last quarter of the 17th Century to the end of the first quarter in the 19th, or for a period of 150 years, all had a bore of approximately .75 inch[6] except for the Musketoon which had a bore of .66 inch.[7] Colonial smoothbores, as distinguished from their purely military arms of European manufacture, had calibers ranging from .70 to .75.[8]

That the smoothbore was the favorite firearm of the Indian is well known, but his reason for preferring it have been grossly misunderstood. The Indian chose the smoothbore between the years 1750 and 1850 not because of stupidity or ignorance, but because during that particular period in the development of firearms it was the most practical hunting gun for his purposes.

One important reason for this preference was that the fusil was light in weight and easily carried; another, that it could be used as a shotgun. But the most important reason of all was that, at the close ranges he normally hunted, it had a shocking power equalled by few of the rifles of that period.

Since the shocking power of any gun depends upon one half the weight of its ball times the square of its velocity, those who belittle the smoothbore must assume that the rifle compensated for its lighter ball by an increased powder charge. An examination of the breech sections of these ancient fusils indicates that most of them also were capable of carrying any reasonable overload. Therefore, a factual discussion of the relative merits of the respective firearms must take into account the relative bore sizes and the ranges at which they were normally employed.

Actually, the reputed inaccuracy of the smoothbore is based upon tradition and heresay. The only real attempt to check this question was made by the late Hampton W. Swaine and reported by Hanson.[9] Swaine used an 18th Century smoothbore and a Northwest Gun in his experiments. Loading the guns with 2½ drams (150 grains) of FFG powder and two balls (George Washington advocated a ball and three buckshot for the most effective load) he kept his shots within a 12 inch circle and got 2½ inches of penetration in a pine board. Using a single ball, the groups averaged 6 inches at, apparently, 45 yards. This hit a card measuring 9 x 7 inches. Presumably, these balls were patched with bed ticking, for, by way of comparison, a 4 inch group at 100 yards is respectable shooting with a round ball rifle of that period, but using modern sights which adjust for windage and elevation!

When viewed objectively, then, it seems that the trade fusil, though a relatively inexpensive gun and well adapted to the manufacturing techniques of the time, was a very practical firearm under conditions of the extreme frontier. When patched, that old smoothbore could deliver the ball with surprising accuracy and effectiveness; certainly as accurately and as effectively as the time and place demanded.

1. Peterson (1956), ARMS & ARMOUR IN COLONIAL AMERICA, p. 46.
2. ibid., p. 14.
3. ibid., p. 48.
4. Russell (1957), GUNS ON THE EARLY FRONTIER, pp. 22-24.
5. Hicks (1938), NOTES ON FRENCH ORDNANCE, 1717-1936, p.9
6. Peterson (1956), ARMS & ARMOUR IN COLONIAL AMERICA, p. 165.
7. ibid., p. 170.
8. ibid., p. 179.
9. Hanson (1959), THE INDIAN FUSIL, The Gun Digest, p. 128.

V
BIBLIOGRAPHY

BIBLIOGRAPHY

ANONYMOUS
   1819 *Cyclopedia or Universal Dictionary of Arts, Sciences and Literature,* London.
ANONYMOUS
   No date. *The Story of Fort Atkinson.* Washington County Historical Society, Fort Calhoun,
      Nebraska.
ARCHER, H.G.
   1905 Oldest British Industry, *Los Angeles Times,* Sunday Magazine Section, May 28.
   1906 The Oldest Industry in England. *The Wide World Magazine,* March, pp. 527-533.
BAKER, EZEKIEL
   1835 *Remarks on Rifle Guns.* (London) Reprint edition, Huntington, W. Va.
BANNERMAN, FRANCIS, *et al.*
   1955 *Catalogue of Military Goods,* New York.
BARSOTTI, JOHN
   1956 Mountain Men and Mountain Rifles, *The Gun Digest Treasury.*
BEERS, HENRY P.
   1956 Mountain Men and Mountain Rifles. *The Gun Digest Treasury.*
BERRY, B., C. CHAPMAN and J. MACK
   1944 The Archaeological Remains of the Osage. *American Antiquity,* Volume 10, pp. 1-11.
BROWN, CHARLES E.
   1918 Indian Trade Implements and Ornaments. *The Wisconsin Archaeologist,* Volume 17,
      No. 3.
CHAPMAN, CARL H.
   1946 A Preliminary Survey of Missouri Archaeology; Part I, Historic Indian Tribes. *The
      Missouri Archaeologist,* Volume 10
   1959 The Little Osage and Missouri Indian Village Sites, Ca. 1727-1777, A.D. *The Missouri
      Archaeologist,* Volume 21, No. 1.
CHAPPELL, PHIL E.
   1902 Missouri Village, *Malta Bend Oui Vive,* June 6.
   1906 *A History of the Missouri River,* Kansas State Historical Collections, Volume 9.
CLARK, RAINBIRD
   1935 The Flint Knapping Industry of Brandon. *Antiquity,* p. 43.
CUTBUSH, JAMES
   1814 *American Artist's Manual, or Dictionary of Practical Knowledge,* Philadelphia, Pa.

DEANE, JOHN
   1858 *The History and Science of Fire-Arms,* London.
DIDEROT
   1778-
   1781 *Encyclopedia,* Paris.
DILLON, JOHN G.W.
   1946 *The Kentucky Rifle,* New York.
DOLOMIEU, CITOYEN (DEODAT BUY SILVAIN TANCREDE GRATET DE DOLOMEIU)
   1797 Memoire sur l'art de tailler les pierres a fusil *(silex pyromaque). Journal Des Mines,*
      tome 6, No. 33, Prairial, An 5, pp. 693-712. Paris.
EVANS, ARTHUR J.
   1887 On the Flint Knappers' Art in Albania. *Journal of the Anthropological Institute of
      Great Britain and Ireland,* Vol. XVI.
EWERS, JOHN C.
   1956 The Northwest Trade Gun. *Alberta Historical Review,* Volume 4, No. 2, pp. 1-7.

GARRARD, LEWIS H.

1955 *Wah-To-Yah and The Taos Trail,* Norman, Oklahoma.

GEORGE, J.N.

1947 *English Guns and Rifles.*

GILLET-LAUMONT, F.P.M.

1797 Extrai d'un memoire du Citoyen Salivet, sur la fabrication des pierres a fusil dans les departemens de l'Indre et de Loir-et-Cher; avec l'indication de quelques autres lieus ou il s'en fabrique egalment. *Journal Des Mines,* tome 6, No. 33, Prairial, An 5, pp. 713-722, Paris.

GLENDENNING, IAN

1951 *British Pistols and Guns, 1640-1840.* London.

GLUCKMAN, ARCADI

1948 *U.S. Muskets, Rifles, and Carbines.* Buffalo, NY.

GOODING, S. JAMES

1956 A History and Listing of Canadian Gunmakers. *The American Rifleman,* April.

GORDON, ROBERT B.

1959 "Early Gunsmith's Metals", *American Rifleman,* December, pp. 32-34.

HANSON, CHARLES E., JR.

1955 *The Northwest Gun,* Publications in Anthropology, No. 2 Nebraska State Historical Society.

1959 "The Indian Fusil," *Gun Digest,* pp. 126-128.

HARVEY, WILLIAM

1947 Britain's Oldest Industry. *The Rifleman,* Summer.

HAWKER, PETER

1826 Instructions to Young Sportsmen . . .

HICKS, JAMES E.

1937 U.S. Military Shoulder Arms 1795-1935: The Smoothbore Flintlock as a Military Arm, *Journal of the American MIlitary History Foundation,* Vol. 1, No. 1, Spring.

1938 *Notes on French ordnance, 1717-1936*

1939 *Firearms, 1702* (Memoirs D'Artillerie by Pierre Surirey de Saint Remy).

1940 *Notes on U.S. Ordnance,* 2 Volumes.

1957 *U.S. Firearms, 1776-1956,* La Canada, California.

HILL, ED C.

1914 Has the Site of Fort Orleans been Discovered? *Missouri Historical Collections,* Volume IV.

HILLARY, JOHN T.

1803 *The Birth of Armament Industry in France,* London.

HOWELL, CLEVES H.

1958 American Military Rifles. *The Gun Report,* Vol. III, No. 12, Aledo, Ill.

JOHNSON, SALLY A.

1956 Cantonment Missouri, 1819-1820. *Nebraska History,* Volume 37, No. 2.

1959 The Sixth's Elysian Fields: Fort Atkinson on the Council Bluffs, *Nebraska History,* Volume 40, No. 1.

KIVETTE, MARVIN A.

1959 Excavations at Fort Atkinson, Nebraska: A Preliminary Report, *Nebraska History,* Volume 40, No. 1.

KNOWLES, FRANCIS H.S. AND ALFRED S. BARNES

1937 Manufacture of Gunflints. *Antiquity.* Volume XI, No. 42, pp. 201-207.

LEWIS, BERKELEY R.

1956 Small Arms and Ammunition in the United States Service. *Smithsonian Institution Miscellaneous Collections,* Volume 129.

MATTISON, RAY H.

1951 Old Fort Stevenson, a typical Missouri River Military Post. *North Dakota Historical Quarterly,* Vol. 18, No. 2-3, pp. 1-40, Bismarck, North Dakota.

MAXWELL, MOREAU S.

1959 Archaeological Investigation of Fort Mickilimackinac, Preliminary Report. (Hectograph), The Museum, Michigan State University, East Lansing.

MAXWELL, MOREAU S. AND LEWIS H. BINFORD
    M.S. Excavation of the Fort Mickilimackinac Site, Mackinaw City, Michigan: First Season—1959.

MAYER, JOSEPH R.
    1939 Early Virginia Gunlocks. (Reprinted from American Collector) *Rochester Museum Occasional Papers and Reprints,* Rochester, N.Y.
    1943 Flintlocks of the Iroquois, 1620-1687. *Research Records of the Rochester Museum of Arts and Sciences.* No. 6, Rochester, New York.

PARSONS, JOHN E.
    1952 Gunmakers for The American Fur Company. *New York Historical Society Quarterly,* Volume XXVI .

PARSONS, JOHN E. AND JOHN S. DU MONT
    1953 *Firearms in the Custer Battle,* Harrisburg, PA.

PETERSON, HAROLD L.
    1956 *Arms and Armour in Colonial America,* Harrisburg, PA.
    1956 a. The Care of Antique Firearms. *Gun Collectors Handbook,* The National Rifle Association, Washington, D.C.
    1959 b. The Development of Firearms, Parts 1 to 4. *Gun Collectors Handbook,* The National Rifle Association, Washington D.C.

PLENDERLEITH, H.J.
    1956 *The Conservation of Antiquities and Works of Art,* London.

POLLARD, HUGH, BENNET, C.
    1926 *A History of Firearms,* London.

ROBERTS. NED H.
    1940 The Muzzle Loading Cap Lock Rifle, Harrisburg, PA.

RUSSELL, CARL P.
    1944 The Trade Musket. *Muzzle Blasts,* Volume 5, No. 10, Portsmouth, Ohio.
    1957 Guns on the Early Frontiers, Berkeley, California.

SALIVET, CITOYEN (LOUIS GEORGE ISAAC SALIVET)
    M.S. Unnamed manuscript report submitted to the Administration Des Armes Portatives of the First Republic in the Year 2 (1793-94). (Not seen by translator) Abstract in Gillet-Laumont, 1797, pp. 713-719.

SMITH, CARLYLE S.
    1950 European Trade Material from the Kansas Monument Site. *Plains Archeaeological Conference News Letters,* Vol. 3, No. 2, pp. 2-9, Lincoln, Nebraska.
    1954 Cartridges and Bullets from Fort Stevenson, North Dakota, Plains Anthropologist, No. 1, pp. 25-29.
    1955 An Analysis of the Firearms and Related Specimens From Like-A-Fishhook Village and Fort Berthold I. *The Plains Anthropologist,* NO. 4.

SMITH, G. HUBERT
    M.S. Excavation of the Site of Ft. Pierre II (39ST217). Missouri Basin Project, River Basin Surveys, Smithsonian Institution, Lincoln, Nebraska.
    1954 Archaeological work at 32ML2 (Like-A-Fishhook Village and Fort Berthold) Garrison Reservoir, North Dakota, 1950-1954. *Plains Anthropologist,* No. 2, pp. 27-32.

STEELE and HARRISON
    1883 *The Gunsmith's Manual,* (Republished by Thomas G. Samworth, 1945 and Gun Room Press, 1977.)

STEEN, CHARLIE R.
    1953 *Two Early Historic Sites on the Southern Plains.* Texas Archaeological Society, Bulletin, October, 1953. Austin, TX.

THAYER, B.W.
    1947 a. Features Distinguishing the Hudson's Bay Musket. *The Minnesota Archaeologist,* Volume 13, No. 2, pp. 34-35.
    1947 b. Features Distinguishing the U.S. Fur Trade Musket. *The Minnesota Archaeologist,* Volume 13, No. 2, pp. 36-37.

THWAITES, R.G.
    1899 *The Jesuit Relations and Alllied Documents,* Volume 43, Cleveland.

TOMLINSON, CHARLES
    1852 *Cyclopaedia of Useful Arts and Manufactures.* 2 volumes, London.
TONNELIER, CITOYEN
    1797 Unnamed manuscript submitted to the Societe Philomatique. (Not seen by translator) Summarized in Gillet-Laumont, pp. 719-722.
TRUMBULL, JOHN
    1934 Orderly Book. *Bulletin of the Fort Ticonderoga Museum,* Vol. III, No. 3.
WILSON, THOMAS
    1899 Arrowpoints, Speaheads and Knives. *Annual Report of the United States National Museum, for 1897.*
WINANT, LEWIS
    1952 *Pepperbox Firearms,* New York.
WOODWARD, ARTHUR
    1951 Some Notes on Gunflints. *Military Collector and Historian,* Volume III, No. 2, pp. 29-36. (Reprinted in this volume.)
    1953 Spanish Trade Goods, *The Sobaipuri Indians of the Upper San Pedro River Valley* by Charles D. Peso. The Amerind Foundation, Inc., No. 6, Dragoon, Arizona.
WRAY, CHARLES F. and SCHOFF, HARRY L.
    1953 A Preliminary Report on the Seneca Sequence in Western New York, 1550-1687. *Pennsylvania Archaeologist,* Volume 23, No. 2.